CASSELL STUDIES IN PASTORAL CARE AND PERSONAL
AND SOCIAL EDUCATION

D1322935

DRUGS: PARTNERSHIPS FOR POLICY, PREVENTION AND EDUCATION

Other books in this series:

CASSELL STUDIES IN PASTORAL CARE AND PERSONAL
AND SOCIAL EDUCATION

DRUGS: PARTNERSHIPS FOR POLICY, PREVENTION AND EDUCATION

A Practical Approach for Working Together

Edited by
Louise O'Connor, Denis O'Connor
and Rachel Best

CASSELL

Cassell
Wellington House   PO Box 605
125 Strand   Herndon
London WC2R 0BB   VA 20172

First published 1998

British Library Cataloguing-in-Publication Data
A catalogue record for this book is available from the British Library.

ISBN 0–304–33945–8 (hardback)
    0–304–33946–6 (paperback)

Typeset by York House Typographic Ltd, London
Printed and bound in Great Britain by Redwood Books, Trowbridge, Wiltshire

Contents

Series editors' foreword

In an age when the emphasis is upon the formal school curriculum, and the demonstration of 'school effectiveness' in terms of the kinds of learning outcomes which can be easily measured and published, the work which schools do to promote and sustain the well-being of their students as fledgling citizens is too easily ignored. Nor does the value of multi-agency work in addressing pressing social problems receive the attention it deserves. This is curious, since much is said (and written) by those who generate social and educational policy about the fear of breakdown in society's norms and values and of the role which schools must play to protect the core values of society. It is just that we seem to have great difficulty in thinking about both the instructional and socialization functions of schooling at the same time!

Effective pastoral care encompasses both the case work teachers do with individuals who find themselves in difficulties of one sort or another, and the pastoral curriculum of SMSC (spiritual, moral, social and cultural education), directed towards personal development and individual empowerment. It is the dimension of schooling where the promotion of pro-social behaviour and a concern for those who are the victims of (their own and others') anti-social behaviour should be brought together not just to minimize undesirable behaviour but to promote the personal and social growth of all our youngsters.

For maximum effectiveness, schools' efforts need to be harmonized with the efforts of other agencies. A clear understanding of how different agencies conceptualize and approach social problem areas, informed by systematic research and evaluation, is crucial to this endeavour.

Drugs: Partnerships for Policy, Prevention and Education provides just such a perspective. In focusing in particular upon the potential of collaborative work by schools, health authorities, the police and other agencies through such mechanisms as the Drug Action Teams (DATs), the potential for more effective collaboration in response to the drugs issue is clearly established. Moreover, this book should raise awareness amongst teachers and others concerned with education of the need for better communication and closer collaboration in areas of social concern generally. We are delighted to include this book in the series.

Ron Best
Peter Lang

Foreword

Roehampton Institute London has a long and distinguished tradition of vocational commitment to education, training and development of the caring professions, including teaching, health care and therapeutic work. Through its four constituent colleges, this commitment has been developed and extended through key partnerships with charitable, religious and voluntary bodies and public and private sector organizations, to address major concerns of communities and society.

One of the key concerns has related to the increasing prevalence of legal and illicit drugs at all levels, in inner cities, urban areas and the shire counties. The increased availability of drugs is linked with the increase in young people's drug use and misuse, and the decrease in age of first experimentation. Clearly, this is of concern to all individuals and agencies with a mission to protect the health, welfare and safety of young people and the communities in which they live. It is to support those individuals and agencies at the forefront of delivering the objectives of the White Paper *Tackling Drugs Together* that Roehampton Institute has facilitated partnerships in drugs research, prevention and education.

This book is the result of a number of collaborations which have focused on how to move drugs strategies forward in the light of research evidence and reflections on professional practice. Thus the authors are drawn from policy makers and practitioners across the fields of education, health, local authorities, police, drugs agencies and research. The chapters arise out of collaborations in research projects and prevention/education initiatives undertaken at Roehampton Institute London within the Faculty of Education, supported by the Addictive Behaviour Centre.

The Addictive Behaviour Centre and the Faculty of Education continue to work with external agencies to develop graduate and post graduate training and gather research evidence to inform the ongoing needs of drugs workers and educators in the field and their clients. *Drugs: Partnerships for Policy, Prevention and Education* exemplifies how higher education can use the special skills of scholarship to inform practical action addressing problematic drugs issues.

Professor Stephen Holt
Rector, Roehampton Institute London

Acknowledgements

Thanks to Professor Ron Best for his help and support in getting this project off the ground; Patricia O'Connell for her assistance in the typing and general production of the book; Tanya, Denis and Annabel O'Connor for their forbearance and support throughout the writing and editing of this book.

Contributors

David Best is Clinical Research Psychologist at the National Addiction Centre, Maudsley Hospital and Consultant to the Faculty of Education, Roehampton Institute London.

Rachel Best is a Research Assistant in the Department of Psychology, London Guildhall University.

Tony Blowers is the Chairman of Surrey Drug Action Team, Member of Council of the Psychiatric Research Trust, and Vice-President of the Hospital Saving Association.

Colin Chapman is Drugs Education Co-ordinator, Redbridge Drug and Alcohol Services, and Visiting Lecturer to the Certificate in Drugs Prevention and Education, Roehampton Institute London.

Roy Evans is Assistant Dean with responsibility for research in the Faculty of Education, Roehampton Institute London, and Project Director for the National Evaluation of School Drugs Policies (Home Office).

Vivienne Evans is Education and Projects Manager for The Advisory Council on Alcohol and Drug Education (TACADE).

John Grieve is Deputy Assistant Commissioner, Anti-Terrorist Branch, New Scotland Yard. He is an Honorary Fellow of Roehampton Institute London and a Member of Council for the Institute for the Study of Drug Dependence.

Jane Mallick is a Research Associate in the Faculty of Education, Roehampton Institute London.

Colin Martin is a Researcher in the Addictive Behaviour Centre, Roehampton Institute London, and a practising Addictions Counsellor. He is a member of the Signpost Community Substance Misuse Team, London.

Jenny McWhirter is a Senior Research Fellow in the Health Education Unit, School of Education, Southampton University.

Filiz Mortimer is Patient Liaison Officer at King's College Hospital, London, and has recently completed an MSc in Health Education and Health Promotion at Southampton University.

Denis O'Connor is Assistant Commissioner (South West London), Metropolitan Police, and is an Adviser to Roehampton Institute London on drugs prevention and education. He is a member of the Police Foundation independent inquiry into the UK Drug Laws, supported by the Prince's Trust.

Louise O'Connor is a Senior Research Fellow at the Roehampton Institute London, and Director for the collaborative research project between RIL and the ACPO (Association of Chief Police Officers) Drugs Sub-Committee.

Jenny Rowley is the Young Persons' Programme Manager for the Specialist Health Promotion Service, Merton, Sutton and Wandsworth Health Authority.

Georgina Stein is a Senior Lecturer in the Faculty of Education, Roehampton Institute London, and is currently on secondment to the AZTEC Digital Learning Centre.

Noreen Wetton is a Senior Research Fellow within the Health Education Unit, School of Education, Southampton University.

Paul Wotton is an Inspector in the Community Safety and Partnership Policy Portfolio Unit, New Scotland Yard, Metropolitan Police.

Introduction

Louise O'Connor and Denis O'Connor

Given the devastating impact on individuals and communities of substance misuse, there are excellent reasons for establishing well-planned national and local strategies in drug prevention and education. The Conservative government White Paper *Tackling Drugs Together* (1995) provided a framework for all public sector organizations to collaborate in this area, through the provision of Drug Action Teams (DATs) set up by District Health Authorities from September 1995.

Within the White Paper, drugs education for young people is recognized as a central plank of a wider prevention policy, with guidelines on drugs policies and education issued through the DfE circular *Drug Prevention and Schools* (1995) and the DfE/SCAA publication *Drug Education: Curriculum Guidance for Schools* (1995).

The election of a Labour government in June 1997 has resulted in a preliminary review of drugs policy and practice co-ordinated by the Central Drugs Co-ordination Unit (CDCU). An extensive refocusing of objectives and strategy is expected once a newly appointed (by the Prime Minister) UK Anti-Drugs Co-ordinator, entitled 'Drugs Tsar', is in post. However, Ann Taylor, chair of the government's Drugs Committee, has already signalled this government's aversion to taking any route to legalization in an article in *The Times*, 'Why this Government won't legalise drugs' (29 August 1997).

The Foreign Secretary, Robin Cook, has further indicated this government's approach to illegal drugs by announcing that the SAS, MI6, MI5 and police and customs will assist Third World countries to address soaring production and the related increase in trafficking to Britain and the rest of Europe. Nevertheless, such determined stances by the government are taken against a backdrop of increasing public and media debate about drugs, with some calling for legalization in the absence of apparent failure to exercise control. Despite this, a Royal Commission has been ruled out, a gap which has effectively been filled by an independent inquiry launched by the Police Foundation. Backed by the Prince's Trust, the two-year investigation will review and examine the workings of the 1971 Misuse of Drugs Act.

However, the articles presented here indicate that there are no 'quick fix' solutions, and that no single response is likely to succeed on what is a multi-faceted, complex problem. For example, there would appear to be problems in developing co-ordinated and coherent approaches which utilize the talents and resources of all concerned professionals. Possible reasons for this, identified from the literature, include poor communication between key agencies, differing philosophies, conflicting priorities, and failure to identify a consensus view on the best course for action.

Furthermore, partnerships formed from the key agencies are threatened by uncertainties surrounding organizational change and resource difficulties in the public sector. It could be argued that the infrastructure to deliver the key objectives of the White Paper (1995) has been weakened rather then strengthened by these.

Nevertheless, there are a number of promising developments which could inform strategy in this field. These include agreement at national (government) level, across all key departments, on the White Paper's *Statement of Purpose*, namely,

To take effective action by vigorous law enforcement, accessible treatment and a new emphasis on education and prevention to:

- increase the safety of communities from drug-related crime;
- reduce the acceptability and availability of drugs to young people; and
- reduce the health risks and other damage related to drug misuse.

In addition to providing a clear national framework for prevention and education strategies, the White Paper encourages DATs to build on good practice wherever it exists at local level, and to gather data which will demonstrate progress on the key objectives.

The White Paper is a new combination of efforts attempting to link enforcement, treatment and education. It provides a focus in terms of both priorities and measurement and, perhaps most importantly, it provides a new infrastructure in the shape of DATs for partnership. The pedigree of the 'British approach' is underlined with a new stress on the respectability of treatment, and the recognition of the failure of discrete approaches, involving undue reliance on enforcement. It recognizes the importance of local solutions to local problems. Above all it stresses the need for practical action now.

Those who doubt the scale of the problem should examine the relentlessly rising statistics for seizure of heroin, and the falling prices. The public are bombarded with the problem, as the *Guardian* of 29 March 1997 reports: 'Childline said that they had come across cases of children as young as eleven with heroin problems. There were many in the 14–18 age group.'

The drugs problem has leapt up the scale of public concerns to rival burglary and violent crime as a top priority, as a survey for *Which?* magazine has demonstrated (August 1996). Realistically it is too early to say whether the new multi-stranded approach will make a significant difference. The mixture is an act of faith with no working model elsewhere to draw upon. Nor are there a collection of accredited tactics that are known in combination to turn the tide. The dynamics of drugs markets are still poorly understood, and a worry remains that there will be a time-lag in mobilizing all the elements required. But this approach is the best prospect we have; all others are either too risky or proven to be counter-productive.

This book is aimed at identifying the issues that are emerging as we try to work together on practical schemes in the classroom and beyond. It is intended to help accelerate the learning cycle for those who are engaging the issues practically: as one contributor puts it, 'time is not on our side' (Chapter 2). We have asked each of our contributors to remind us briefly of the value of the particular element they are addressing, what we know about how it might impact on the problem, and their experience of engagement with it at this stage. All contributors have the virtue of being practitioners: their observations are revealing, sometimes troubling, but ultimately optimistic that we can progress.

PART 1
Policy, Prevention and Education

CHAPTER 1

Intelligence as education for all? Government drugs policies 1980–1997

John Grieve

I have been arguing for some time that the police are only stopping an escalating drugs problem getting substantially worse. This is increasingly difficult, increasingly risky – physically to young people and to many others including my close friends policing the streets or working in drugs agencies, and socially to us all. To what extent has current government policy been informed by police intelligence over the last seventeen years?

As the American writer Abram Shulsky[1] has said, one role of an intelligence officer is to educate his or her customers. I want to provide a police intelligence perspective on which to base our discussions about our role *with* (not necessarily but potentially in) schools and colleges. A task of intelligence is also to inform policy makers and to provide strategic information. We also provide tactical or operational information at a local level: this is what is described as the 'information base' for partnerships in giving advice on best practice. This is a move towards some aspects of police intelligence becoming open. The juxtaposition of the words 'open', 'source' and 'intelligence' produces shudders from some of my police colleagues.

There have been four published public UK government total strategies for drugs. The most recent White Paper, *Tackling Drugs Together* (1995)[2] proposed stronger frameworks founded on the principle of partnership. This policy involves vigorous law enforcement, education and prevention. It includes increased safety, reduction in health risks and reduction in acceptability and availability.

The White Paper also discussed community damage limitation (although this is a phrase many people dislike). This can be seen as an emphasis on prevention and education to increase the safety of communities, particularly in respect of young people; and on active leadership and management through the role of the 105 Drug Action Teams (DATs) (as O'Connor and Blowers argue in Chapter 2 below) and their supporting Drugs Reference Groups (DRGs). These forums provide roles for all members of society to contribute to local solutions to local problems as the basis of real partnerships. Strategic leadership at this level has the potential to reduce conflict, ensure balance of power, and provide resources, accountability and evaluation. The twelve new, larger Home Office Drugs Prevention Initiative Teams act to support the DATs in all these areas.

The partnership element was present in earlier strategies and can be assisted by Intelligence. Intelligence was specifically mentioned in the government strategy but not necessarily in its widest definition of 'information designed for action' (a phrase I owe to Jennifer Sims).[3] The collective and individual information needs of DATs are a paradigm of an intelligence requirement. Information designed for an action might also be a use of the term *education*. Two other crime concepts are useful in the wider debate: reactivity is 'action against the drug problems'; proactivity is 'action in respect of individuals' (both the latter phrases I owe to Brian Greenan).[4]

'Harm reduction principles are not incompatible with vigorous street policing. Indeed in many circumstances they actually require it and the wider communities concerns would certainly be served by vigorous focused street level policing', said the Advisory Council on the Misuse of Drugs (1994).[5] This seems excellent good sense, but needs to be fuelled by information. We have come a long way despite the huge increase in the problems we face. At the end of the 1970s police strategy was firmly enforcement, supervision of licit supply and pursuing the dealers; it was beginning to have an intelligence strategy. But the 1980s were to be another decade of change: changed structures, changed tactics, changes in the nature of dealing and international drug trafficking, and of course major statements of changes in policy. In 1980 in the UK the Parliamentary Home Affairs Select Committee on Hard Drugs[6] was directed to examine expenditure, administration and policy of the Home Office and associated public bodies: this was to form a pattern for the decade.

The year 1980 also showed the furtherance of a European perspective. The Pompidou Group, a co-operation group to combat drug abuse and illicit trafficking in drugs, allied itself to the Council of Europe and set up a small permanent secretariat (the member states were those of the EEC plus Norway, Sweden, Turkey, Spain, Portugal and Switzerland by 1986). It also had observers from such diverse places as the Vatican and, surprisingly, by 1986 included Hungary.

In 1980 the UK acknowledged the role of money in the drugs business, and the Hodgson Committee was asked to look at profits of crime and their recovery. This Committee was set up in the wake of *R* v. *Cuthbertson* (1980), the famous Operation 'Julie' a major undercover LSD investigation. The Bill for the Confiscation of the Proceeds of Drug Trafficking based on the *Hodgson Report* was published, and achieved royal assent in 1986. The strategy was to link drugs, money and people. The legislation identified new offences, powers, restraint orders, confiscatory fines and international dimensions. The idiot's guide to the Act involved the number three. The Act contained three new offences, took effect at three stages, and created a Section 3 statement, whilst placing liability on three bodies. The money-launderer uses a three-part process: placement when the money goes into the system, layering when it is concealed and moved about or washed, and re-integration when it reappears as 'clean' money. Many criminals use small businesses to introduce the money. The pool of dirty money, however, contains more than just drugs money: it includes stolen aid money, tax avoidance, fraud, arms and grey money. In London, police set up the first substantial programme in the UK to introduce new skills to tackle the investigative problems. If I had been writing then, I would have been optimistic, but – though positive aspects of teamwork have emerged, including partnerships and information flow – it has not been as successful as I would have predicted. I do not know why not, unless the answer lies elsewhere than with money.

Part of that answer may have been in a paper published the same year, the ACMD, *Treatment and Rehabilitation* report[7] which

1. defined the subject as a 'problem drug user' as opposed to the previous emphasis on addicts;
2. identified the need for resources, both in statutory and in non-statutory agencies; and
3. highlighted the increasing pressure for local responses to local drugs problems, to which Regional Health Authorities were responding, by providing Drug Problem Teams, advisory committees, clinics, advice and counselling.

Licensing, prescription, research and training were also recommended by the report. The DHSS advised all Regional and District Health Areas and Authorities to explore the size of the problem and provide local treatment.[8] This was the beginning of the development of local indicators, a development in which the police showed considerable interest as the concept emerged of local solutions to local problems.

On the world stage a major development in 1983 was the posting by the UK of a National Drugs Intelligence Unit Officer to Amsterdam. A Customs Officer was posted to Karachi. These were the first two of the UK Drug Liaison Officers, and demonstrated to the world that an intelligence structure was coming into place. A Metropolitan Police detective was the first police incumbent.

But even more fundamental changes in the police's actual investigation of the economic bases of the drug problem were under way in the UK. A Committee under Ron Broome, Chief Constable of Avon and Somerset, reported on 28 May 1985[9] and recommended a three-tier approach to the problem and the setting up of the Regional Drug Wings 'back to back' with the crime side of Regional Crime Squads.

The Police contributed significantly to the Home Office report *Tackling Drug Misuse*.[10] As a summary of the government strategy, it was a unique document in crime strategy terms. No other report has had such a strategic thrust and description. In the Metropolitan Police Service (MPS) by 1983 we were actively pursuing partnerships and local initiatives in south London, in particular thanks to the innovative work of a local drug prevention leader, Jud Barker and others in Southwark.

The report of the Home Affairs Committee on the Misuse of Hard Drugs[11] made seven recommendations in respect of intensified law enforcement efforts: these concerned the role of armed services, seizure, forfeiture of assets, international banking secrecy as a problem, laundering of cash, posting police officers abroad, increase in penalties for trafficking to life, trial in the UK for UK-related offences, crop eradication and substitution policies.

How does all this compare with the 1995 strategy for partnership in information sharing? The position is that strategy is rooted very firmly both in the formative work of the 1980s and in local communities. Local DATs are just that, users of information designed for action. Police strategy through local Drugs Reference Groups produces drug problem profiles of localities both in collaboration with other local groups to supply information for use locally and by other national agencies. What we have now really are local solutions to local problems. This is not so much about different levels of tolerance of drugs in different communities as about hard decision making in a time of limited resources and escalating demand.

One of the police's priorities is drug-related violence. We seek priorities locally arrived at, so that everyone has shared ownership in the possible solutions. This avoids unfulfilled expectations. The aim is jointly to reduce damage to communities and to assist in reducing demand to relieve the social pressure that fuels demand on the dealers. A good day for police enforcement is a day when the problem does not get any worse: it is local education and local prevention schemes that will actually tackle a social problem of amazing complexity. Some people, of course, will always see such local drugs strategies as no more than a holding exercise unlikely to make a lasting difference. There is no reason why this should be the case, as proved by the King's Cross Operation 'Welwyn', a multi-agency approach designed to reduce prostitution, drug dealing and related crime in the early 1990s.

Intelligence, I have written, is 'designed for action': the tools of intelligence can be described as a cyclical process involving collection of information, its evaluation, the development of the initial findings – for example more surveillance, more information from 'open sources' of intelligence, analysis of those findings, dissemination to those who need to know and action leading back to further collection plans. You rarely start from nothing.

Where did all this local intelligence drive come from? We had a mandate from our Commissioner within a few months of his appointment in 1993: 'Surveillance, targeting, intelligence, informants and things that will give us a better chance of catching criminals in the act'.[12] This was based partly on the Audit Commission's proposals to make the police more proactive. Catching local drug dealers in the act involves understanding the whole range of environmental, social, economic and educational factors. These local problems vary immensely in complexity from one Operational Command Unit (OCU) to another, owing to the interaction between the kind of street drugs concerned (of which there are many), the individual street criminal or misuser, the immediate situation in which the drugs are taken or the crime occurs, and the culture or subculture in which the situation has given rise to it. This is the DISC (drugs, individual, situation, culture) model, an acronym based on the first letters proposed by the Advisory Council on the Misuse of Drugs, which provides a context for examining the meaning of drugs to individuals and communities.[13]

Two recent European initiatives point up the development both internationally and generally of open source intelligence. The Institute for the Study of Drug Dependence is the operational end in the UK of the European Monitoring Centre on Drugs and Drug Abuse (the Home Office is the policy end for the UK). The other is the European Association for the Treatment of Addiction. Both provide Europe-wide analysis and comparative data on an open database to any customers.

On the enforcement side in the UK, arrests of dealers have gone up, at a time when our procedures for convicting people have been ever more complex not least through disclosures made in court in the presentation of evidence. Operation 'Crackdown' is a Metropolitan Police operation against drug dealers in the line of 'Bumblebee' (burglary) and 'Eagle Eye' (streetcrime).[14] In London we used to average out six to one users to dealers arrested. Our strategy was never aimed at users, and this apparent anomaly is explained by each dealer generally having more than six customers. The users are caught up either in our operations against dealers or because they come to notice during other police activity as we make the peace on the street. Our focus is the robust pursuit of the significant dealers while not ignoring the fact that use is (still) a crime.

Intelligence has indicated for some time that drug use, as well as being a crime, itself causes crime. Tony Newton, then Leader of the House of Commons and the government lead on drugs policy, said in June 1996 that 664 drug misusers between them committed seventy thousand crimes.[15] The street value of illegal drugs seized nationally in 1995 amounted to £457 million, 5 per cent up on 1994. The number of drugs offenders was up 25 per cent to 87,000. The only debate is about the proximity or otherwise of the casual links. Drug use is a crime in itself, it leads to organized crime by its transactional international nature, it leads to violence, it leads to acquisitive crime. The causal connection is sometimes incredibly complex: it is rarely obviously immediate and it is often confused by a range of other factors. Drug use and/or dealing can accelerate at a tremendous rate. Drug users whose crimes have been examined include those who have chronic opioid, cocaine or amphetamine use and are likely to become involved in crime and to accelerate their use.

Leaving crime to one side, there is the role of the family or friendship networks in drug use and dealing. Children are more likely to be offered drugs for the first time by a member of the family or a close friend than by the archetypal dirty-raincoat-attired stranger at the school gates. School parents' associations who call on the police to arrest the dealers fail to realize that it is often their own children and their classmates they are referring to, as recent ecstasy tragedies and inquiries have shown. Recreational or leisure routes, for example through clubs and raves, allow drugs to flow. These networks seek to minimize the risk of police activity. The networks are essentially chaotic with some patterns, and can be disrupted, as the London drugs policy has shown, by local action involving police, strong management in the clubs and a robust attitude to dealer networks.[16]

Drugs cannot be kept out of these islands, and the police's various allies who attempt to do this now do not wish to be held responsible alone. Our own Customs, despite record seizures of drugs worth over £1 billion in 1994, warned of a drug war they could never win alone.[17] By 1996 the Customs were reporting an increase of 80 per cent in heroin seizures between 1994 and 1995.[18] This would have provided 658 million medical dosages. Before the integration of Germany, while the Berlin Wall and Iron Curtain were still in place, with minefields, barbed wire, military corridors and four armies camped around Berlin (all the ingredients here for a war on drugs), there was still a drug problem in the Kreuzberg and Zubahnhof regions. The Berliners were not growing opium poppies or coca in the city. None of us should be seeking external causes alone for the problems of our own society; the causes, and the solutions, are here in our homes, in our schools, in our localities, in our communities and hence inside our own heads.

Partnership is rewarding police work. It is the core of the Metropolitan Police strategy and good practice guidelines published in March 1996. It goes to the heart of our work and experience, with the first vehicle of expressions of social disgust for drugs being the S.106 Police Community Consultative committees. The DATs are the second important vehicle to express our social disgust. These two strands contribute, for example, in the following ways.

Education. In May 1996 the Metropolitan Police re-emphasized the long-standing role of the police schools involvement officers in total health education packages. The supply of current information to schools – teaching the teachers, parents, governors – was updated with a video, *Pack of Truths*,[19] and new written material for use with 12 to 14 year-olds. The aim of having a consistent policy in place to deal with drug incidents before they occurred had been achieved with almost complete coverage of schools in London. Projects aimed at the culture and situation (as the DISC model showed) involving older young people have concentrated on public houses and then on clubs and raves. One of the most successful partnerships is with the London Drug Policy Forum, who shared with us their best practice for safety at clubs and dance venues, ranging from advice on how to deal with dehydration to thwarting organized dealers.[20]

Harm reduction. The police's original involvement with needle exchange schemes and HIV/AIDS awareness has led, through involvement of local officers on DATs and Reference Groups, from physically picking up needles to improving all local facilities. Other areas where harm reduction has worked are clubs, dance venues and public houses, as I have already described.

Research. Besides Howard Parker *et al.*'s cohort study,[21] which is quite the most important longitudinal current research on the drug-using behaviour of young people in the north-west of England, some of the most interesting and innovative research has been informal unreported work by sixth-formers amongst their peers. Police are contributing to the development of knowledge on the nature of local and wider area supply networks. Police work with the victims of drug-related violence is also extremely important in underpinning that knowledge and undermining the tactics of dealers.

Cautioning policies. Despite some recent adverse publicity in respect of rock stars and obvious variations from place to place, cautioning is having an effect in individual causes of drug misuse (going back to the DISC model again). The potential link with street agencies and cautioning schemes is powerful (there were eleven such agencies counted on one Metropolitan division!). The most recent studies suggest that broadly conceived social problem referral schemes (following cautioning or court action) covering housing, money and general health as well as drug problems are more effective than limited specialist drug referral. Information on the effectiveness of cautioning and referrals will be vital to inform DATs and help direct their investment.

Media strategy. This is important for encouraging the spreading of accurate information. (An example is the ISDD media awards – one category was recently won by local reporters on local solutions of local problems.) Police are seeking alliances in our work with youth for positive role modelling and spread of good practice, for example alliances with the licensed victualler press[22] for spreading policy and sharing best practice, values and information.

Joint training. Training for citizenship, personal safety and physical risk reduction has been given by the police in a variety of places, in collaboration with other agencies, including education and health. Training for schools involvement officers in the police has been delivered by Health and Drug Education Co-ordinators funded by local authorities. The government strategy and Drug Prevention Initiative (DPI) emphasize the cross-cultural benefits of such joint training. However, an explicit requirement for successful joint training is the trading of *intelligence between agencies*, a process some find more painful than others.

The increase in the problem of drug use suggests that we are exercising only minimal intervention in respect of existing users. We can effect more powerful intervention before children start using drugs. As many people have said, the best policy is not to start. With our communities we *can* work to maximum interventions with the dealers. That is why education for all is so important.

Since 1980 my position has veered between optimism and pessimism. Enforcement alone has not solved and will not solve the drugs problems. The best the police can do is to disrupt the drugs trade. The effort involved in remorselessly pursuing dealers across the globe, tackling their supply networks and risking violence while at the same time using the same intelligence for education and informing policies, should not be underestimated.

Open intelligence as education has to be even-handed, otherwise it tends towards dogma, propaganda, censorship of the unwelcome or indoctrination. Education must come from teachers, parents, peers and school governors. Educating young people is a specialist task that can be informed by police intelligence. It can be direct, or part of wider programmes or it can inform the educators.

Law enforcement has only effected minimum intervention with established users. It can effect maximum intervention with dealers and in partnerships. Partnerships based on an accurate information base can effect maximum intervention in education. Quite frankly partnership and social mobilization based on open intelligence are our last chance. The Commissioner of the Metropolitan Police called this a crusade.[23]

NOTES

1. J. Sims, 'What is Intelligence?' (paper 1) in A. Shulsky and J. Sims *What is Intelligence?* (Working Group on Intelligence Reform, Consortium for the Study of Intelligence, Georgetown University, 1993).
2. White Paper, *Tackling Drugs? Together*, CMD 2846, (London: HMSO, 1995).
3. J. Sims, 'What is Intelligence?'
4. B. Greenan, unpublished SID discussion paper 9MPS, CID, SO110.
5. Advisory Council on the Misuse of Drugs, *Drug Misuse and Criminal Justice* part II (London: HMSO, 1994).

6. House of Commons, *Report of Home Affairs Committee*, 1982/12.
7. Advisory Council on the Misuse of Drugs, *Treatment and Rehabilitation* (London: HMSO, 1982).
8. *Report of Home Affairs Committee*, 1982/12.
9. R. Broome (chair), *Report on Drug Enforcement Arrangements* (ACPO UK (unpublished), 1985).
10. *Tackling Drug Misuse* (London: HMSO, 1983).
11. *Report of Home Affairs Committee*, 1982/12.
12. *Panorama*, BBC TV, April 1993 and *Daily Telegraph*, 3 February 1994.
13. *Treatment and Rehabilitation*.
14. MPS, *Drug Strategy/Good Practice and Policy Guidance* (DPA, Metropolitan Police, 1995).
15. Hansard (1995), 2 June 1996.
16. *Dance till Dawn Safely* (London Drug Policy Forum, PO Box 270, Guildhall, London EC2 P2EJ); *Independent* (London), 29 January 1997; *Licensee and Morning Advertiser*, 12 September 1996.
17. *Daily Express, Daily Telegraph* (London), 4 August 1994.
18. *Evening Standard* (London), 1 May 1996; *Evening Standard* (London), 10 February 1997; *Evening Standard* (London), 17 March 1997.
19. Metropolitan Police, *A Pack of Truths*, video and teachers' pack for secondary schools (1996).
20. *Daily Express, Daily Telegraph* (London), 4 August 1994.
21. Parker, H., Measham, F. and Aldridge, J. (1995) *Drug Futures: Changing patterns of drug use amongst English youth.* Monograph 7, London: ISDD.
22. *Licensee and Morning Advertiser*, 17 June 1996.
23. Commissioner of Metropolitan Police, press conference 16 May 1996.

CHAPTER 2

Drugs: making a difference through Drug Action Teams

Denis O'Connor and Tony Blowers

A house divided against itself cannot stand . . . our cause must be entrusted to, and conducted by its own undoubted friends – whose hands are free, whose hearts are in the work – who do care for the result.[1]

INTRODUCTION

Lincoln articulates for us the need to build a strong and enduring alliance if we wish to engage truly the great challenge in front of us. The introduction of Drug Action Teams (DATs) recognizes and stresses the need for building strong interpersonal relationships and bonds. If they operate well they can enable each of us in our own agency or walk of life to know how other partners will respond in any given situation: for example who will have a tendency to get the job done, or, if pressed, procrastinate and delay; who can be counted on in emergencies; who is most committed; and which people share a strong performance ethic in reducing abuse of illegal drugs.

It is, of course, early days – DATs were set up only in 1995. It's been a time of conferences, plans, exchanging ideas and learning about one another. It really is too early to judge whether 105 DATs will 'measure up', as one recent article put it, but it is not too early to take a view on whether they are likely to succeed.[2]

THE POTENTIAL OF DATs

The remit of the DAT as outlined in the 1995 White Paper *Tackling Drugs Together* was to

draw up an action plan to tackle the drug problem in its area; ensure that the respective organisation policies and operations (of the various agencies) are in line with each other; ensure that a Drug Reference Group is established and operates effectively; and make progress in line with the Statement of Purpose and national objectives in the light of local needs and priorities.[3]

The *Statement of Purpose* was intended to be a key driver in directing effort. This is specified in *Tackling Drugs Together* as being:

to take effective action by vigorous law enforcement, accessible treatment and a new emphasis on education and prevention to:

* increase the safety of communities from drug-related crime;
* reduce the acceptability and availability of drugs to young people; and
* reduce the health risks and other damage related to drug misuse.[4]

Senior staff from all the key agencies (health, police, education, social services, prisons, probation, Customs and Excise) were designated to form DATs – that is, to create and serve them.

This, for those who remember the late and unlamented District Drugs Advisory Committees, is both an ambitious working arrangement and an ambitious programme of work. Politicians of all main parties have put weight behind this approach and symbolically pledged to co-ordinate the great departments of state to promote progress.

Plans were required by March 1996 and have been under way for over a year at the time of writing. Updates and progress were under review by the Central Drugs Co-ordinating Unit (CDCU) in March 1997. What was this likely to reveal? Examination of even a small sample of plans is likely to show significant variation in style and in the senior staff and the agencies attending the Drug Action Team meetings. Most plans that we are aware of point in the same direction as the statement of purpose. However, they vary quite substantially in terms of the depth to which they pursue each of the individual elements: some may have seven or eight priorities, others in excess of forty. Chief officers from key agencies do not always attend but the meetings do attract senior players from the key agencies, who should be able to speak with authority and assist in decision making.

There are a number of frustrations to overcome: some were predictable and have been rehearsed in other articles on partnership.[5] They include:

* converting data on drug problems into 'information for action' by DATs. Even if they get past issues of complexity and confidentiality, the intelligence base of agencies is partial and, if developed at all, is not oriented to resource joint activities (see J. Grieve in Chapter 1 above).
* establishing what are effective services. The report of the Task Force to Review Services for Drug Misusers, which studied and reported in parallel with the White Paper *Tackling Drugs Together*, is the best reference document we have. It was intended to inform the Department of Health in producing guidelines for purchasers of drug services. It usefully includes an assessment of services from counselling to rehabilitation and, importantly, a *measurement framework* that covers issues of drug use, physical and psychological health, and social functioning.[6]
* assessing and establishing new services, for example for addicted offenders or young people. This means cutting into existing budgets, assuming that the need can be properly identified in these cases. The establishment of need is a recurring theme: this is an area where perhaps the CDCU could highlight best practice to avoid each DAT attempting individually to determine from scratch how this should be done.

- making headway where best practice is uncertain (for example education programmes in schools, where there are a lot of confusing and apparently contradictory messages and programmes currently operating). Reference to professional bodies (for example the Association of Chief Police Officers) and guidelines by key institutions (such as the Department for Education and Employment) may be helpful, if DATs wish to avoid being caught up by fashionable but unproven endeavours.

An emerging issue is the question of the degree of *executive authority* of DATs. There is a feeling abroad that they do not have executive authority, and some take this to mean that their principal purpose is to act as a catalyst or to ensure alignment between the agencies and the avoidance of conflict. The difficulty is that this approach will not take us very far forward, since the drugs problem is not organized around the remit of particular agencies and has flourished in the past while each agency has brought its own particular approach to bear on the problem. The danger is that DATs could end up 'being in place but not in charge'. This is a more worrying prospect than any of the significant predictable issues referred to above, and could rapidly undermine the perceived value of DATs. The essence of it is that DATs can have as much executive authority as the members are willing to invest in a common endeavour: the problem certainly requires executive action, and, if DATs fail to take it, they will fail.

HIGH-PERFORMANCE DATs

Given the obstacles to be overcome, it is unlikely in our view that DATs operating as a 'loose group' rather than as a 'team' are likely to wish to use executive authority. Without being seen to be united and grappling directly with the problem, their image or profile will be weak – they will not give the lead to others.

We need to be quite clear on this: if DATs were intended only to enable individuals in agencies to do their jobs well and to swap notes on good practice and ideas, then a committee or working group approach is much more comfortable, less risky and less disruptive than trying to build and perform well as a *real team*. But the thrust of *Tackling Drugs Together* is more ambitious than that; success relies not primarily on the sum total of individual contributions, but on multiplying the combined effort of all. The indications are that many of the critical tactics in dealing with drugs involve integrating services. Examples include: a 'crackdown' on drugs, making prescribing services available for addicted offenders caught; linking police, health care workers and teachers in drugs education programmes in schools; and connecting prison, social and health services to provide aftercare for addicted prisoners on release.

A useful model is encompassed in *The Wisdom of Teams*.[7] Based on a detailed study of fifty different teams operating in thirty companies, the book describes how committees and groups may progress to become teams, but highlights the point that merely calling a group a 'team' does not make it one. They define a team as: 'a small number of people with complementary skills who are committed to a common purpose, performance goals, and approach for which they hold themselves mutually accountable'. Each element of the definition is significant, and all are required for successful teams. Let us consider each in turn.

Small number. Most DATs operate with ten to twelve members (but some have up to twenty). Most are not so large as to prevent the constructive engagement and intervention associated with smaller management groups – so size should be no problem. Some DATs allow decisions and actions to be taken where five members are present; this enables the momentum to be maintained.

Complementary skills. The study found that the right mix of complementary skills is necessary to do the job, including functional skills, problem-solving, decision-making and interpersonal skills. The important functions are represented on DATs as intended in *Tackling Drugs Together*, but problem-solving and interpersonal skills may or may not coincide with those formally represented. The point seems to be for each DAT to be aware of the need, make its own assessment and give preference in commissioning work to those acknowledged to have the requisite skills, rather than to those in the formal positions of chairman, co-ordinator and so on.

Commitment to common purpose and performance goals. In as much as plans exist for each DAT, the first test of this aspect is superficially met. The first batches of plans vary, however, in relation to the degree to which they are based on joint intelligence (see J. Grieve in Chapter 1 above) and specify the measures by which their success can be tested and their monitoring regime. DATs have used a variety of methods to generate support around their intentions, varying from the inclusion of alcohol addiction in their remit to the provision of special briefings for opinion formers such as MPs and seminars for stakeholders. It is hoped that the current range of objectives on educational issues, youth services and addicted offenders will add some sense of urgency and perhaps a fear of failure, and provide a focal point for the DATs' efforts. As we shall see, the ultimate test as to whether there is a 'common purpose' will be in the degree of effort given to achieving the results sought in the plans: this will indicate whether they are a shopping list or a set of firm and shared intentions.

Commitment to a common working approach. Teams need a common approach in working together. This involves a number of social and cultural dimensions, but includes a willingness to take on work, and to decide who will do what job, how schedules can be set and how decisions will be made and changed if necessary. If the approach confines all real work to a few members and allocates joint effort only to review and discussion, then team levels of performance will not be achieved. This is because, in large measure, there is no *collective work product to supplement individual performance.* Of course there are different agendas at work here, given the pressure members bring from their 'day job' outside DATs; for example, Health Authorities and LEAs (Local Education Authorities) are under severe financial pressures, and different agencies work at different speeds. This aspect requires investment and a measure of patience, but not indolence. For instance, the 'can-do' culture of the police may jar with the more deliberative, consultative way in which business is done within healthcare. The concern with the *individual* treatment by health and social services may sit uncomfortably with the team responsibility for the *community* impact of drug misuse. Other policy or cultural clashes already faced by DATs include the priority given to referrals from the Criminal Justice system, including direct referrals from police stations and treatment recommendations from the courts, and local objections to needle exchange schemes. Real teams will find a way of bringing these tensions to the surface and accommodating them successfully.

Mutual accountability. This is perhaps the most demanding test. The difference is perhaps between the attitudes 'the DAT chairman holds us accountable' and 'we hold ourselves accountable'. As the authors of *The Wisdom of Teams* comment, 'the first case can lead to the second: but without the second there can be no team'. If the second applies it will be because there is a clear measure of commitment and trust by those involved. If the players hold themselves accountable for the team goals, rather than a particular individual action, then a contract exists where they can properly and reasonably express their own views about all aspects of the team effort and expect those views to receive a fair and constructive hearing. For example, at an early stage in the planning cycle, when members of the DAT discuss their own agency strategies, it is worth posing the question whether those strategies could be changed following consultation with partners. For instance, if the police put forward their strategy on the basis that it might be changed, then the *quid pro quo* may be that a similar flexibility could be expected of prisons, Customs & Excise and so on. It is also probably foolish to imagine that trust and commitment remain constant and undiminished over time. There are bound to be highs and lows as frustrations and tensions over achievement and ways of working divert individual members from their common purpose and performance goals at times.

CONCLUSION

Most of those who are involved with DATs are familiar with teams. The purpose of describing the model above is to show that if we are honest we are often imprecise in how we think about them. 'Drug Action *Team*' was not an accidental title. Our view is that having a clear understanding of what a team is and what it is not, and particularly of how teams and performers depend on each other, will help to perceive the difference between those that work and those that do not. Our view is that DATs will need to move from being 'groups' to being genuine 'teams' if they are to realize their potential. A useful indication, now that DATs are through the first cycle where the less threatening issues of getting to know one another and exchanging information have already passed by, will be whether members feel comfortable with the rate of progress, whether they feel unified and willing to defend and market collective action. Much will depend on whether they have set themselves significant performance challenges as opposed to useful, but non-threatening, seminars and awareness-raising initiatives. Perhaps the real test will be the establishment of new services and a collective decision to discontinue existing services. Ultimately they will either share a common performance ethic or shy away from it. As the statistics elsewhere in this book bleakly demonstrate, the challenge we face is one that requires a fearless pursuit of performance and change by DATs, not merely playing safe. It is not unreasonable to put the challenge that drugs put on society on a par with the challenge Lincoln faced.

In that context we should accept Lincoln's wisdom that unity equals strength and will be demonstrated by real teams who come forward with real solutions.

NOTES

1. Lincoln's remarks from 'A House Divided' speech in accepting nomination for US Senator at the Republican State Convention in Springfield, Illinois (16 June, 1858).
2. Jane Mounteney, 'One Year On – DATs How Have They Measured Up?' *Drug Link*, July/August 1996.
3. White Paper, *Tackling Drugs Together*, CMD 2846 (London: HMSO, 1995), p. 30.
4. *Tackling Drugs Together*, p. 7.
5. E.g. *Drug Abuse and Misuse. Developing Educational Strategies in Partnership* R. Evans and L. O'Connor (eds), Roehampton Institute Occasional Papers 1. (London: David Fulton, 1992), p. 70.
6. The Task Force to Review Services for Drug Misusers, *Report of an Independent Review of Drug Treatment Services in England* (London: Department of Health, 1996), p. 4.
7. Jon R. Katzenbach and Douglas K. Smith, *The Wisdom of Teams* (Cambridge, Mass.: Harvard Business School, 1993).

CHAPTER 3

The role of parents in drugs education

Roy Evans, Jane Mallick and Georgina Stein

INTRODUCTION

The rights and responsibilities of parents as partners to their children's socialization and education have been recognized in every major educational reform of the past two decades and given particular force in legislation since the Education Act of 1988. Implications for the governance of schools include the requirements that they should make available to parents such information as may reasonably be required to make an informed choice. Such information would normally include an insight into the policies and practices in support of personal safety and healthy development.

Informing parents of school policies and involving them in their development wherever feasible is a recognition of the dynamic relationship which exists between two potent institutions in the life of a child.

Whilst the home and the school can combine powerfully to promote learning and socialization, they do not always work towards similar social goals. Parenting practices and family values do not inevitably result in a reinforcement of the attitudes and behaviours that schools view as significant. To some degree, as we shall show in this chapter, this may be because parents simply do not know what schools do; it may also be because their own needs as parents have not been met. These needs are various and frequently go beyond the quest for appropriate information. Drug prevention initiatives which recognize the crucial role parents can play nevertheless often have to function with inadequate knowledge of the kinds of support parents themselves require if they are to have the confidence and competence to be active partners. Research in this area is relatively sparse.

The purpose of this chapter is to explore briefly the outcomes of a parents' needs survey across a large County Authority in south-east England. Our intention is to deal mainly with the level of understanding that parents claim to have of drug prevention initiatives and resources within local schools and communities, and the extent to which such knowledge is based on personal experiences of involvement. The parents themselves build a vision of more accessible support, a vision which carries implications for programmes of community action which seek to mobilize and empower key agencies, including families, in a collective approach to the prevention of drug abuse.

Despite the significance of parents to the socialization and education of their children, the development of effective parent-involving strategies within prevention-oriented drug education initiatives has been relatively neglected in practice. The research literature on evaluated interventions is sparse, even though parental participation is widely espoused as an essential component of a multi-faceted approach. We would observe, however, that it is not just parent programmes that are under-developed. Much work within schools in pursuit of the recommendations contained in *Drug Prevention and Schools* (DfE, Circular 4/95) is still in its early stages and, as O'Connor *et al.* (1997) point out, there is little evidence as yet that coherent co-ordinated school programmes are resulting from multi-agency approaches. An evaluation of emerging models of drug education policy development is currently under way through the sponsorship of the Central Drug Prevention Unit at the Home Office, but findings will not be available until mid-1998.

Whilst drug education strategies raise particular issues for parents with regard to the health, safety and social behaviour of their child, programmes which seek to involve parents deliberately within educational actions have received relatively little systematic attention, nor have such efforts been routinely evaluated. The research literature that does exist has been reviewed by Evans *et al.* (1997) and is not repeated here. Outside of the field of drug education, however, substantial experience has been gained of involving parents in educational and multi-professional actions in areas such as disability, special educational needs and early childhood services. Effectiveness of provision within such areas has been shown to be contingent upon *co-operation* between different services and families, *co-ordination* of services and *communication* between stakeholders.

Home literacy programmes provide good evidence of the value that can be added by parents to the development of their children when their confidence as home tutors is enhanced. When parents are provided with even basic guidance on how to help children read, subsequent school progress can be considerable. In other contexts, research (e.g. Evans and Robinshaw 1995) shows how parents of children with severe sensory impairment can make a substantial difference to their child's acquisition of communicative competence provided that support exists to *model* appropriate parenting, to *counsel* them through times of uncertainty and to *support* their needs for information at a level they can accommodate.

Within an overall strategy for encouraging children and young people to adopt healthy lifestyles and develop risk-free social habits, the power of parental involvement as a potential force for positive change is increasingly advocated. Too little, however, is known about the breadth and depth of parents' knowledge of drugs, the concerns they experience as their child moves through each phase of the education system and their confidence in their own ability to contribute to preventive strategies. Equally unclear is evidence from parents themselves regarding the kinds of knowledge they regard as worthwhile and the form it should take.

The findings reported below have emerged from a study commissioned to explore the ways in which parents of school-age children in a large County

Authority describe their concerns, and reveal important facets of their own knowledge, awareness and attitudes to drugs, drug use and drug education strategies.

SOURCES OF DATA

In September 1996 one hundred parents of children in years 9 and 10 in each of twenty schools were invited to take part in a questionnaire survey. The schools represented a one-in-six sample of all secondary schools in the LEA and were chosen to provide a balance across a number of school type factors. Principally these were: LEA versus GM or Independent; selective versus non-selective; single-sex versus co-educational; urban versus rural. The enquiry was conducted with the approval and consent of the LEA and with the active participation of the schools. Questionnaires which aimed to reveal aspects of parents' knowledge and concern over drugs and drugs issues, the availability of support services and sources of advice and guidance were sent to them via pupils. To offset the legendary unreliability of 'pupil post', the questionnaires were distributed to the target groups by their teachers, to whom they were subsequently returned in sealed envelopes. Confidentiality was assured at all times. Opportunity for parents to record their readiness to take part in a subsequent follow-up telephone interview was available on the questionnaire with space for noting an appropriate number. Telephone interviews were undertaken with a hundred parents chosen at random from those who expressed a willingness to be contacted. These were recorded with the knowledge of the interviewee and subsequently transcribed and analysed. The response to the questionnaire enquiry was almost precisely 50 per cent, with around a thousand completed questionnaires returned.

Focus group interview sessions were also arranged with parents from six LEA secondary and feeder primary schools to provide opportunities for parents to talk freely about their concerns and their knowledge of support available. These group sessions were also recorded and subsequently transcribed and analysed.

FINDINGS

Extracts from the findings of the main research are presented here for the light they shed on parent's capacity to support local drug education strategies effectively. The comprehensive analysis has been presented elsewhere (see Evans, Mallick and Stein 1997).

It is probably true to suggest that each generation of parents finds reasons for anxiety in contemporary activities and cultural trends. What is significantly different in respect of drugs issues is the fear which exists in respect of illegal substances for the risks of fatality they are seen to pose. In this study parents clearly wish to be part of a solution to the problem as they recognize it. Equally clearly they identify a number of crucial factors which inhibit their capacity to act effectively. Some they view as intractable problems.

Parents talking to their children about drugs

Our interview data identify *the generation gap* as a real obstacle for some parents, which becomes confounded with *difficulty in communicating*.

Half the time they tell you more than you know anyway.

I think just communicating with teenagers about anything is difficult really. It's probably not just drugs ... general communication is not easy at that age.

Kids find it quite hard sometimes to talk openly, perhaps would go to someone else rather than their own parents.

O'Connor *et al.* (1997) found that 56 per cent of young people report that they would turn to a friend if they had a drug problem, compared to only 28 per cent turning to a parent. On the other hand, parents' responses to our questionnaire indicate that fewer than 3 per cent admit to never talking to their children about drug issues.

- Over 97 per cent of parents surveyed report that they 'sometimes' (73.5 per cent) or 'frequently' (23.9 per cent) do talk to children on this subject.

Nevertheless, parents in this study report that the *starting points* for such conversations tend to be fortuitous and opportunistic, although for some there are more specific triggers to discussion:

I mean different things crop up on the television or in conversation or in the papers and we tend to talk about them then. We are quite open about talking about drugs but, as I say, unless anything actually comes up we don't sort of sit down and actually have a talk.

My main concern is to simply to try and create an open and non-confrontational relationship with my child about drugs and drug use. Sometimes I feel inadequate and clumsy in my attempts to discuss the subject but still obviously feel it is important to have some sort of communication.

We talk about it quite often very openly. I think it tends to be when it is triggered by something that we've seen on TV or we've read in the newspaper or if they've been talking about it at school.

We infer that parents' effectiveness could be improved through:

- structured and resourced opportunities for discussion of drug issues.
- developing non-confrontational and non-controversial interactional styles.

Well I think we're the ones that have a real feeling of what the kids think and at what stage they are at and what they need. I think we're the first line of communication with them or we should be. I am obviously doing something drastically wrong.

You can't tell somebody about drugs if you don't know nothing about it.

Parents' knowledge of school-based drugs education

I certainly think you need to know what your children are being taught at school or what information is being imparted so that you can build upon it, discuss it, know about it.

For the majority of parents, school is a place where they feel that drug issues should be discussed with their child(ren). This is overwhelmingly the case at secondary stage, but over half the parents surveyed felt that this was appropriate also at primary school. Their actual knowledge of the policies and practices adopted by their children's school with respect to drug education was nevertheless incomplete. Schools in this sample vary in the degree to which they ensure parents are made aware of their drugs policy and how it is delivered. Some schools do organize information evenings for parents and organize talks by professionals. Others send information to the homes. Taking into account the results obtained from telephone follow-up interviews and focus group discussions with parents of primary and secondary age pupils, we find these schools to be few. On the whole the evidence of real and sustained efforts by schools either to inform or to involve parents is poor.

- 91 per cent of parents agree that it is either 'extremely' or 'very' important to them that their children should learn about drugs issues.
- 94.1 per cent of parents think drugs issues *should* be discussed with their children at secondary school. 57.8 per cent also include primary school.
- 73.8 per cent of parents know that teachers talk to children about drugs issues.
- 40.8 per cent of parents *do not know* if people other than teachers talk to children about drugs issues.

Parents who are aware that the school invites other professionals to assist in the delivery of the drug education programme often acquire this information through their children:

He came home and told me that somebody had come into the school and I can't remember – I think it was the police actually. I think it was somebody else but I know somebody had gone in and given a lecture on it.

I'm not sure about what the schools actually do because me son hasn't sort of come home and said to me – we did this and that today, that sort of thing.

- 65.9 per cent of parents report that either they *have not been* informed of how the school helps children understand drugs issues (42 per cent), or they *are not sure* (23.9 per cent).

I don't know how much drugs education my children have had since they've been here. It is not something they come home and share with me.

No we have had nothing. We get letters through but we haven't had anything through as regards drugs – what they do instructional-wise. No we haven't heard anything at all.

The two girls are still at junior school – I don't thing that they have anything on it. I'm pretty sure because we usually get letters if there is anything slightly controversial that they are going to be spoken to about.

- 75.1 per cent of parents *do not know* the main message that the school gives out about drugs (e.g., 'say no', harm reduction etc.).

I know that they have got a policy but what actually it is I don't know. I do know they have got one.

I would assume they have no policy. Well they obviously have no policy that anybody outside the school is aware of anyway.

Our data show that, of the 24.9 per cent of parents who stated that they knew what the school's 'message' was in respect of drug education, 19.7 per cent believed it was 'say no'.

- 66.8 per cent of parents *do not know* what their children's school does if any child is found with drugs.

Conversely, 33.2 per cent of parents responded that they did know what the school does if a child is found with drugs. Of these parents, 80.3 per cent chose not to respond to the request to specify the action the school would take. The remainder who did usually responded in terms that stated or implied 'exclusion'.

I guess they are expelled.

I think it's expulsion but I think sometimes they take them back.

- 79.5 per cent of parents *do not think* that they are sufficiently included in drug prevention strategies generally.

Our data show that parents want information in respect of the signs and symptoms of drug use, drug types and their effects on children's health; 88.3 per cent of parents are of the view that drugs issues should be discussed in the home. They note also their need for assistance in developing appropriate strategies to use in discussing drugs with children as well as when and how to introduce the subject.

As parents we can't make the schools teach everything. We've got to take responsibility ourselves. We can't blame the schools for the children taking drugs if we are not prepared to teach them ourselves.

I believe it would be possible to run evening classes at Adult Education Centres where parents could attend, talk about various addictive substances . . . what to do, and how to handle the situation.

Parents frequently referred to feelings of inadequacy based on their own perception that their children were probably better informed that they were: 49 per cent of parents in this study report receiving some advice and guidance through schools – 27.6 per cent report attending a parents' evening and 15.8 per cent refer to a newsletter from the school; 34.9 per cent of parents report having received advice and guidance from alternative sources.

We did have a talk from the person who gave the drugs talk to the children on what to look for – they do it every year.

We had a police officer come in and that was quite informative.

Two over-arching issues emerge from this data regarding parents' perceptions of the schools' role in drug prevention initiatives. First, the issue of *communication with parents*. Broadly this appears less developed than it could be, thus limiting the effectiveness of parents through the inadequate knowledge they say they possess of school policies and practices. As noted earlier, parents are frequently not aware of what happens in school unless their child tells them. Whilst some schools are acknowledged by parents as being active in communicating with the home, the majority of parents surveyed do not evidence the kinds of involvement that 'partnership' may imply. Such partnership as does exist appears weakly articulated and essentially school-driven, leaving parents unsure of the role they could play and unable to support the 'message' on drugs that underpin their child's drugs education. There is little systematic evidence that parents themselves have contributed to drugs policy development or that their values and needs have been actively embraced by the schools.

I'm really quite disappointed at the communication between the school and the home. I think it is because she attends quite a large secondary school ... because of the number of pupils it limits their ability to actually communicate.

My child seems confident that there is adequate education on drugs given at school but, as a parent, I feel too ignorant and would welcome talks by the school.

I don't know specifically what they learn about. I mean she's brought home I think in the whole time she's been at secondary school one leaflet.

Second, there is an issue connected with *how proactive schools are perceived to be* in drawing parents in to support their own drug prevention strategies. Parents want schools to take a lead, but they want also to be involved.

I think that schools who do not, or will not, admit their school has a problem put all our young people at risk.

At the moment you get lots of different teachers with different ideas and some will follow things through and others won't ... something more structured for everybody, parents and children is needed.

The theme of *involvement* recurs:

I think there should be evenings where effects and problems of drugs should be discussed. Also they should get professionals to come in and talk to us – parents and children.

I would like more information for myself and, I think actually, joint training with parents and children.

The only venue I can think of really is within schools, because I can't see any other area where parents and children are kind of like welcomed really.

The parents in this study construct a basic message:

Parents recognize the important role they should play in drugs education. To be effective in this respect requires that

- their own need for information and education on drug issues should be recognized;
- they should share a perspective with the school on the message to reinforce;
- they should acquire skills in communicating on sensitive issues, and have access to appropriate resources.

Parents see schools as significant institutions in facilitating their own development as well as the development of their children. This would require, however, more clearly focused and purposeful strategies of involvement by schools than we find evidence for in the current survey.

Parents' knowledge of community-based services and resources

I would go to Yellow Pages, I think. Look it up under 'D'.

- 76.5 per cent of parents are not aware of what services exist in their area to help them in relation to drugs issues.

Those parents who stated that they were aware of other services made reference to their GP, a drug helpline, specialist drug services and the police. Parents report that if the need arose they would access services through the telephone directory, the Citizens' Advice Bureau or the Samaritans. Proportionately more parents in selective schools mentioned the police and their GP, as providers of help with drugs issues.

In a similar way, a relatively higher proportion of selective school parents, 40.4 per cent, reported having received advice and guidance on drugs issues from sources other than the school. For non-selective school parents this figure was 28.3 per cent. The aggregated figure for all parents irrespective of school type was 34.9 per cent. In this sample it is interesting to note, from the information parents provide, that non-selective schools appear to make greater use than selective schools of outside professionals to provide advice on how to deal with drugs issues: 55.1 per cent as compared to 43.9 per cent.

'Parents need to be told what's there really.'

Parents need more awareness of exactly what is available and not just for the kids who are actually involved in drugs.

The biggest service would be to let parents know and children know about what services are available.

As one parent succinctly put it, 'If you don't know the service exists, it is not available to you.' From the parents' perspective, services that exist to provide assistance need to advertise their availability. Additionally parents report that they would find it helpful to have readily accessible points of reference.

- 5.7 per cent of parents report being aware of a drug helpline.

Of parents 47 per cent state that they would find it helpful to have access to a helpline. The advantages of such a service are seen to lie in its complete confidentiality. This is viewed as an important feature of an advisory service.

> Parents wouldn't feel comfortable actually going in to a health promotion unit and asking for advice. Lots of them feel quite intimidated like they do coming into school and places like that. They like the telephone because it's fairly anonymous.

To be useful to parents and children such a service needs to be widely advertised and highly visible in the community.

> I think there is a support line but I couldn't tell you off the top of my head.

For young people the services need to be targeted in the settings they frequent:

> But the places kids hang out are not the Library. You've got to target it at places where kids hang out, at nightclubs . . . have a phone number up on the wall, in the toilets.

- 2.5 per cent of parents report being aware of a drug counselling service.

Parents nevertheless see the merits of a counsellor being available. For some this could most usefully be located within the school. The need for a 'drop-in' service received frequent mention. For others the location is less important than that the service should be accessible to both children and themselves.

- 27 per cent of parents in this survey say they would like to have access to a drugs counsellor.

> A parent shouldn't be isolated with that problem.

> I would like to see them actually situated at the school and readily available for any children at break times – especially lunchtimes they could actually go without having to say to a teacher, please Miss, I want to go and see them.

> Counselling that involves the children and parents together, so that they can all be together and talk about it together, and then maybe get it sorted out.

- 6.5 per cent of parents reported that they were aware of a specialist drug agency in their area. Only 1.4 per cent of parents have ever received advice or guidance from such an agency.

From the interviews and focus group discussions we gain a clear impression that such an agency lies outside of the likely needs perceived by parents of primary school children. On the basis of their limited knowledge of the purpose and existence of such an agency, and their more limited contact with a drug specialist, parents do not see such services as designed to respond to their concerns and fears or to issues connected with infrequent using or experimentation. Although rather more parents recognize their GP and the local health centre as a source of assistance with drugs issues, only one in twelve of the respondents to the questionnaire (8.4 per cent) mentions this directly.

Reviewing the evidence available, our data creates a broad impression of parents who:

- have had little or no contact with community-based services in respect of drugs issues and show poor awareness of how they would access them;
- tend to see use of such services as crisis-led, and thus construe their functions as more to do with remediation than with prevention.

In recognizing the potential value of services directed at drugs issues, parents point to the need for effective marketing of these services so that they are *accessible* when they are needed. Parents also see merit in the provision of opportunities for appropriately resourced discussions led by a professional and attended by the young person along with the parent(s). They recognize the significance of a family focus.

Drugs education and prevention: parents' perspectives on better services to children and families

Parents view substance abuse as a major social problem, an aspect of the culture which at one and the same time is normalized and sensationalized by the media. They show awareness that drug use by young people has no single root cause: they similarly appreciate that the problem is unlikely to be amenable to simple solution. Importantly, however, parents in this study do see themselves as part of a solution. It is clear from our data, through both the questionnaires and the interviews, that parents want more effective strategies of prevention and education, want to be more effective partners to such strategies and have suggestions as how this could come about.

> I would have suggested that there should be a combined effort between school and parents . . . but parents need to be briefed about what's happening at school. I think widely circulated information . . . combined effort.

> Because a lot more can be done when parents and schools work together. I think the school does not have the main responsibility for this, they have a captive audience with the children and have responsibility there, but they don't have the main responsibility. So it is a matter of team work really.

We have been able to infer from the data available to us that parents view themselves as significant agents in prevention and education with respect to drug issues and as partners with schools in their children's development. We find that parents are able to articulate a strong sense of when this process should begin and the message it should convey.

- 57.8 per cent of parents hold the view that drugs issues should be discussed with children at primary school.
- 6 per cent of parents report that they received advice and guidance from their child's primary school on drugs issues.

From the focus group discussions amongst parents of primary-age children we find that for the majority of parents no clear sense exists as to what primary schools did about drug education or what policies existed. We find also that, whilst parents are cautious as to how much emphasis should be placed on drugs issues at an early age, they show a clear sense of agreement that *secondary school is too late.*

- 94.1 per cent of parents hold the view that drugs issues should be discussed with children at secondary school.
- 75.1 per cent of parents of secondary school children *do not know* how schools frame the 'message' regarding drug use.

These findings are significant from two points of view.

First they are *an indicator of the degree* to which parents have been involved in the process of policy formulation by schools. In this respect parental participation is not strongly articulated by schools in general, although the responses of a few individual schools show clearer evidence of co-operation and communication.

> You have to make a school, an open sort of school, where parents can come. I think sometimes people feel that they can't, they're not really school-orientated sort of people. They just send their children here because you have to send your children to school.

Second, they are an indicator of the extent to which parents and schools share a perception of the educational challenge and act in a manner which is mutually reinforcing. We have noted earlier that existing guidance on successful parent–school co-operation is predicated upon the notion that parental values are valid in their own right and have to be accounted for within proposed interventions. As a principal this does not apply *just* to schools. Where parents are involved in the development of policy they become engaged by the discourse, understand the principles on which it is based and are better equipped to act in accordance with these principles subsequently. Parents do not acquire ownership of educational strategies by giving them information. Ownership is acquired through engagement and interaction. The consequences of the low level of such involvement revealed in the present study is exemplified by the findings that, contrary to what schools are encouraged to do through the best advice available to them.

- 39.4 per cent of parents think that children should be taught to 'just say no'.
- 16.2 per cent of parents think that children should be taught that 'drugs kill'.
- 33.4 per cent of parents think that children should be taught the dangers of drug use.

> I am quite concerned about the attitude, in the drugs support world, by some professionals who seem to think that it's inevitable that kids will, and because it is inevitable the only thing we can do is to minimize the damage, and that really worries me because it is giving the kids the message – this is expected of us.

> I don't know why people have such a problem with 'just say no' really.

> It's an absolute no no. It's black and white as far as I am concerned. It's not, 'if you do take them be careful or take a friend along in case'.

The message that was coming across quite clearly at an evening that I went to was 'be careful' not 'don't'.

Parents are fearful for their own child's safety and view with distrust what they think they understand of the 'professional approach'. For many parents, the educational principles underpinning the discourse on 'informed choice', 'personal responsibility' and 'self-determination' do not carry the conviction they need in securing the ultimate safety of their child. There is little evidence in the current data to suggest that parents will have had opportunity to engage in an exchange of views over the approach to drugs education adopted by their children's schools. Moreover, within the data available to us there is little to suggest that they have been actively involved in the development of a community-based approach. Within the range of views expressed by parents, some exist which may be taken as broadly supportive of a more educationally orientated approach to drugs prevention programmes.

Yeah, it's like everything in life – they've got to make a decision and you can't just blatantly say to them 'say no'. You've got to give them the information and they will decide really, because they are going to come to an age when 'just say no!' isn't an option for them. They are going to want to try.

Well, all you can do is, as we are all saying here now, is have as much information as you can on drugs and say, well, this is why you should say no because of all these reasons and then hope, as you say, they make the right decision.

OVERVIEW

There are very evident dilemmas for parents. There are similar dilemmas for professionals in all agencies working towards effective drugs prevention strategies. Research suggests strongly that the 'just say no' approach does not work for children in general. Effective practice requires alternative guiding principles and minimally an agreement on who the client group should be. If parents are to be seen as effective partners, and if families are potentially a powerful force for good, how is their engagement to be ensured?

There are dilemmas here also for different agencies and different professional groups who participate in drug prevention work. Effective collaboration requires co-operation and consultation at every level.

Almost thirty years ago a report of the Carnegie UK Trust Fund enquiring into services for handicapped children noted, 'there are many fingers in the pie, but no cook'. With differing priorities, different codes of conduct, different conceptions of 'client' and differing pressures on resources there is still the risk in multi-agency approaches that the 'cook' has not been identified and that professional actions with regard to parents are neither mutually reinforcing nor effectively targeted. We raise this as an issue only in so far as research on community-based interventions systematically raises co-ordination as an issue which impacts on effectiveness.

Our data do not lead to the view that the parents we have surveyed and interviewed recognize any harmonization of the policies and practices of schools, the police service, social services, the health service or drugs prevention agencies. On the contrary, their recognition of the contribution that each could make is based to a degree on speculative hope, informed in measure by common sense and their own past experiences.

Involving parents in deliberate acts of educational and social intervention is not without its difficulties. Drawing upon a broad base of interventionist research, the present authors have noted (Evans, Mallick and Stein 1997) that in creating the framework for parental involvement professionals need to consider carefully:

- their definition of partnership and the likelihood of parents being viewed as equal partners;
- the ethical requirements of their own service and the extent to which these constrain relations with other services and with families;
- the degree to which their own training and socialization equips them to share perspectives on social issues with other disciplines.

Parents' attitudes to different public agencies are governed by the effects of their own past actions. Similarly, their own life experiences influence their child-rearing practices as well as their attitudes towards children's actions and behaviours. Their effectiveness as partners to social and educational programmes depends on their knowledge of the issues and the skills they can bring to bear. The social ecological perspective leads to the view that changing the behaviour of an individual has to be seen in the context of the social psychological environment of which (s)he is a part. Such changes have to be significant in their effect on behaviour and to endure over time.

- Parents can be helped to become more effective partners through the provision of appropriate training, information and support. Helping parents is, in some circumstances, an essential precursor to helping children.

Of particular significance to all modern institutions is the idea that effectiveness is achieved through investing time and effort in building a vision of the future, attending to issues of communication, developing skills and knowledge amongst participants and working for the achievement of shared values and common understandings. What is necessary within individual institutions is equally relevant when different institutions and organizations are partners to a common venture.

REFERENCES

Evans, R. and Robinshaw, H. (1995) 'Caregivers'' sensitivity to the communicative and linguistic needs of their deaf infants. *Early Child Development and Care*, **136**, 79–94.

Evans, R., Mallick, J. and Stein, G. (1997) *A Study of Parents' Needs in Respect of Drugs Education for their Children*. London: Cedar.

O'Connor, L., Best, D., Best, R. and Rowley, J. (1997) *Young People, Drugs and Drugs Education: Missed Opportunities*. London: Roehampton Institute.

CHAPTER 4

Addiction counselling: working in partnership for the identification and referral of younger clients

Colin Martin

INTRODUCTION

Though much has been written on the *special* difficulties faced by younger people in relation to drug and alcohol abuse (Black 1979; 1982), this perspective also tends to occlude the reality that many of the psychological and social issues pertinent to substance abuse are not age-specific (Churchill *et al.* 1990; Khantzian 1985; Goodwin 1984; Martin and Otter 1996; Mash *et al.* 1993). It is also arguable that perpetuating a belief system that young people face fundamentally different difficulties in relation to substance abuse may restrict this group's access to effective treatment such as counselling or psychotherapy. This chapter will take a broad view of substance abuse interventions. Case material will be used to illustrate the range of problems that can be identified in relation to younger people's substance abuse. From a developmental perspective, it is argued that substance misuse is representative of a pathway of common elements of causation. In this respect age status is unimportant. However, it is recognized that, in terms of referral and accessing therapies and treatment, young people may encounter problems qualitatively different to older adults. This issue is discussed in detail and illustrated with a referral model developed by a Community Substance Misuse Team (CSMT) which emphasized the importance of a multi-disciplinary community approach to young people's substance misuse.

THE MYTH OF AN AGE-SPECIFIC CAUSE OF DRUG USE

It is an important aspect of the work of many CSMTs to establish outreach services to cater for the special needs of the younger client. However, the provision of such services, which for the most part remain poorly evaluated, has led to the notion that young people engaging in substance abuse are somehow different from adults pursuing a similar pattern of abuse. This is not the case. It has been readily established that many older adults seeking treatment for substance abuse problems have a substance abuse history that can be traced back to adolescence (Cloninger *et al.* 1988; Davies 1992). It has further been established that a significant contribution to the development of substance misuse problems at *any* time in the life course is the experience of childhood adversity such as poor relationships with significant others (Hurley 1990) and physical and sexual abuse (Cavell *et al.* 1993; Ireland and Widom 1994). It is clear that such childhood experiences represent 'spent time' in the life course and their influence will be pervasive to the adult personality structure, which will be relatively stable from adolescence onwards (Churchill *et al.* 1990). Under this rubric there can be no identifiable differences in terms of personality factors between younger and older substance misusers. It can therefore be inferred that treatment techniques which are effective with older substance misusers may be readily applied to a generally younger age group. The salient issue here is a difference in *age*, not a difference in *psychosocial* function or *personality* profile. The emphasis on special needs for younger substance misusers that has been generated by the provision of youth outreach teams is essentially a concept which lacks construct validity. In effect, this represents a process of social attribution rather than problem identification. Unfortunately, this position may effectively prevent younger substance abusers engaging in appropriate support and treatment programmes. If younger substance abusers face special difficulties, it would seem that this is purely representative of a problem in engaging services in the first place. Within this framework the special issue is that younger people would appear to have difficulties accessing services that are freely available to older substance abusers.

A CASE STUDY

To establish the need that specialist substance misuse services should be readily available to young people I will use a case example. An 18-year-old woman named Sharon (the name has been changed to protect confidentiality) self-referred to Signpost Community Substance Misuse Team (CSMT) for help with her problem drinking. She had previously been unable to access any other services. On interview it became clear that Sharon had a long history of alcohol abuse. At the time of initial interview her alcohol consumption was close to 200 units per week. She had rarely had an alcohol-free day for the past two years and was chemically dependent on alcohol. She drank on waking in the morning in order to prevent the symptoms of acute ethanol withdrawal. Sharon had made many attempts to cut down on her level of consumption over recent months but had been unsuccessful. Since Sharon lived alone, was unsupported and was also a possible suicide risk, an in-patient detoxification was arranged which would include a psychiatric assessment. Following detoxification, Sharon was discharged from hospital and was seen on a weekly basis with an initial view towards supportive counselling and relapse-prevention work. It became clear during the course of her counselling that Sharon had been self-medicating with alcohol to deal with painful affect associated with early childhood experiences. Sharon agreed to engage in a counselling relationship focused on her complete personal history in order to deal with these distressing experiences and to explore their relationship to her recent heavy drinking. This type of therapy proved successful, and after several months' work Sharon was discharged from her counselling treatment and embarked on a life of sobriety with the assistance of a support network established during her therapy.

It is clear to see in the above example that a 'chat' with an outreach worker in a local café would have been totally ineffective in dealing with Sharon's initial physiological problems (alcohol dependency) and later associated psychological issues.

OPENING LINES OF COMMUNICATION

With the recognition that confidentiality is a crucial aspect of treatment accessibility to substance abusers, it has become clear that many organizations had little understanding of the salient needs of substance abusers (younger and older) generally. In order to raise awareness of these issues Signpost CSMT devised an educational initiative to promote knowledge of referral procedures to our team. The initiative also included a review of the psychosocial literature on substance abuse causation as well as a detailed review of the pharmacology and pathology of alcohol and drug abuse. The organizations targeted to receive the initiative were the local police and local schools. The sessions were conducted by specialist substance misusers, and feedback from both the police and schools was particularly good. Indeed the police requested that a rolling course of the Signpost educational programme should be conducted at the police station in order to allow every serving officer to attend. Feedback from these organizations was used to shape proposed future initiatives and has been extremely valuable in introducing lines of communication between the CSMT and these organizations. This initiative appears to have had a positive effect on referral practices.

As an example of facilitating communication between organizations this initiative proved most effective yet did not in any way compromise client confidentiality. The use of educational strategies to generate communication between interested organizations provides a risk-free means of entering into a common dialogue.

IDENTIFICATION OF YOUNGER CLIENTS

The identification of substance misuse problems in younger people can be gauged by a variety of indices. Accepting that boundaries between them can often blur, these can be broadly grouped into three factors: psychosocial; physiological; and forensic.

PSYCHOSOCIAL FACTORS

Psychosocial factors embrace a broad scope of environmental interactionist elements. However, a useful dichotomy is between family-focused and non-family-focused psychosocial features. It has been established on many occasions that alcohol and drug misuse is strongly predicted by childhood experiences within the family group (Orford and Harwin 1982). These experiences need not necessarily consist of concrete behaviours such as physical and sexual abuse. Issues pertaining to emotional rapport and parental anti-pathy and bonding are also important predictors of adult substance abuse (Mullen *et al.* 1993). It is therefore important to recognize dynamic clues to substance abuse in the context of family relationship discord.

Non-family-focused psychosocial features include those enduring features of personality that are associated with drugs use and the impact of peer relationships and peer group pressures. Undoubtedly, peer group pressures and affiliations are an important contributor to both social behaviour and social identity. It has been established that peer groups are an important facilitator of both adaptive and deviant behaviour (Tajfel 1982). However, anecdotal clinical evidence suggests that during adolescent development the peer group influence on alcohol or drug use is transient, in as much as drug use may be representative of a developmental aspect of a short-lived peer group. Under this rubric, such use of illicit substances may be perceived as experi-mental and time-limited. In effect 'going through a stage' of experimental drug use is described. This example, in the general sense, does not represent a strong case for counselling or treatment interventions and, indeed, inter-ventions applied to this scenario may *facilitate* a problem by implying a non-existent psychopathology.

PHYSIOLOGICAL FACTORS

The pharmacological effects of drugs and alcohol may be pivotal in bringing a drug or alcohol issue within an individual to the awareness of parents or concerned significant others. It has been established that most drugs, includ-ing alcohol, can cause physical pathology following excess use. This mode of physiological damage may be either direct or indirect. An example of a direct effect of physiological damage would be excessive consumption of alcohol. Owing to the specific metabolic route of alcohol, excess consumption can lead to liver damage that can be detected by a routine liver function test. Since the liver may become enlarged, accompanied by referred pain felt in the kidney area, it is likely that this pathology would become noticeable to significant others because an individual is likely to seek medical attention for 'back pain' which a combination of competent medical examination and a blood Liver Function Test (LFT) would reveal to be alcohol-related. The indirect route of physiological damage refers to complicating factors regarding drug use rather than the pharmacological properties of the drug itself. In many ways the indirect mode of physiological harm is of more concern since the associated effects can be equally life-threatening as direct effects but less predictable. A classic example of this would be the case of the injecting heroin user who shares needles. An individual who shares needles is at high risk of a number of life-threatening illnesses and conditions including septicaemia, HIV/AIDS and hepatitis C. Though these are not the result of the pharmacological effect of heroin *per se*, they are the result of a high-risk behaviour associated with injecting heroin. Therefore it is possible that a user may come to the attention of the clinician via one of the associated illnesses rather than as a result of the pharmacological properties of the drug. A further, frequent, example of the indirect route is through accidents occurring to the individual while under the influence.

It is clear that both the direct and the indirect mode of expression are likely to lead the drug user into some clinical contact and/or a situation where parents become aware of a drug problem. It is quite often under these circumstances that contact with a specialist drug counselling agency is made.

FORENSIC FACTORS

Media exposure has done much to highlight the importance of drugs issues to society generally. Though the focus of much media attention has been on drugs smuggling, drug-related murders and drug gangs, it has become clear that, amongst the hyperbole, an individual drug user may come into contact with a counselling agency via the courts. This situation raises an interesting and profound paradox in terms of the philosophy of substance misuse counselling.

The forensic paradox

A significant proportion of individuals seeking help for drug-related problems and attending CSMTs have forensic records, usually for drug possession or supply, or theft to support a drug habit. Quite often the courts will make an order that, rather than being sent to prison, an offender will be given a community service order and ordered to attend a CSMT under the auspices of a probation officer. The problem here is that any worthwhile model of counselling has at its core the need for clients to *desire to change* their lifestyle, including drugs use. From this point of view the decision to engage in counselling should be representative of an informed and free *choice*. It is clear that the position whereby the client is given a choice by the courts of either counselling or prison does not satisfy the criteria for a motivational desire to change from the client. Indeed, this situation is unsatisfactory from both a psychotherapeutic and an attributional perspective – i.e., beliefs about responsibility (Martin and Hewitt 1996). Consider the following scenarios: (1) A man ransacks a pensioner's house and uses a degree of violence. This results in a prison sentence. (2) A man ransacks a pensioner's house and uses a degree of violence; he tells the court that he needs the money to buy drugs because he is 'addicted'. This results in a suspended sentence on the understanding that the offender attends for some counselling. Though the crime and the consequences to the victim are the same in both instances, the attribution of addiction has removed culpability. Clearly there are not likely to be many circumstances where an offender will be motivated to change to being non-addicted since there are so many judicial benefits to being addicted! This situation is completely untenable, of course, and the harm to society is great. I have often heard clients who enter counselling under these circumstances suggest that the only reason they were attending counselling was to avoid a prison term. I'm sorry to say, from my own clinical observations, that this group generally do not progress well in counselling and, almost inevitably, re-offend.

A MULTIDISCIPLINARY INNOVATION

Recognizing the just described situation as highly problemat therapeutic, Signpost CSMT launched an initiative in 1994 in part the local police and schools to try to increase interventions prior to individuals entering the forensic treadmill of substance abuse. The rationale was simple: communicate effectively with front-line services to educate across the borough. This would serve to raise the profile of the CSMT as a resource within the region. A team of Signpost's counsellors and psychologists met regularly with the local police to implement an education package regarding drug-related issues. The police were able to use this information in order to impart knowledge to young people they came into contact with on the streets who might be using drugs and to suggest to them directly resources that were available to them to deal with drug problems in confidence. Feedback from the police was most encouraging. A similar approach was taken with the schools. A Signpost team discussed with groups of schoolchildren issues related to drug awareness and education, and a dialogue with teachers was opened so that teachers could address issues on dealing with drugs issues. Again, as with the police, feedback from both pupils and teachers was very encouraging and appeared to be a vindication of networking the CSMT with other organizations. This experience was strongly suggestive, to our team at least, that multi-disciplinary approaches and working in partnership is an extremely effective means of dealing with existing drug problems and ameliorating potential future ones.

SUMMARY

It is clear from the salient issues addressed in this chapter that drugs or alcohol issues represent the endpoint manifestation of a complex social and interpersonal problem. The drugs issues that relate to younger people in relation to psychopathology are similar to those of older adults, and the consequences of substance abuse are also equally severe. A critique of the efficacy of inexperienced or poorly trained personnel working in outreach teams has been made. Indeed, the author would contest that the use of such outreach workers can lead to serious psychological difficulties being inadequately addressed and vital indicators of physiological harm being missed, with dire consequences.

Further, if we were to agree that it *is* appropriate that poorly trained or untrained individuals are fit to work with younger substance abusers but not older adults, then this also suggests that young people's drug problems both psychologically and physiologically are not as severe or important as those of older adults. This is clearly not the case, and to perpetuate this belief is surely a matter of great conceit. It has been observed that identification of younger clients is crucial if appropriate interventions are to be targeted. It is also crucially important to work in partnership with other agencies to maximize the utilization of such therapeutic resources as are available. Under no circumstances does client confidentiality have to be compromised to achieve these objectives. It has further been emphasized that the current judicial system for dealing with drugs offenders is entirely inappropriate and serves no one's interests, least of all the victim's. A radical review of judicial process in this area is long overdue.

Finally, it should be mentioned that drug problems can be dealt with both satisfactorily and effectively. The mode of achieving this is *always* communication, both within the counselling room *and* within the community at large.

REFERENCES

Black, C. (1979). Children of alcoholics. *Alcoholism Health Research World*, **4**, 23–7.

Black, C. (1982). *It will Never Happen to Me*. Denver, Col.: MAC Publishing.

Cavell, T.A., Jones, D.C., Runyan, R.D. and Constantin Page, L.P. (1993). Perceptions of attachment and the adjustment of adolescents with alcoholic fathers. *Journal of Family Psychology*, **7**, 204–12.

Churchill, J.C., Broida, J.P. and Nicholson, N.L. (1990). Locus of control and self-esteem of adult children of alcoholics. *Journal of Studies on Alcohol*, **51**, 373–6.

Cloninger, C.R., Sigvardsson, S. and Bohman, M. (1988). Childhood personality predicts alcohol abuse in young adults. *Alcoholism*, **12**, 494–505.

Davies, J.B. (1992). *The Myth of Addiction*. Switzerland: Harwood Academic Publishers.

Goodwin, D.W. (1984). Studies of familial alcoholism: a growth industry. In Goodwin, D.W., Van Dusen, K.T. and Mednick, S.A. (eds), *Longitudinal Research in Alcoholism*, pp. 97–105. Boston: Kluwer-Nijhoff.

Hurley, D.L. (1990). Incest and the development of alcoholism in adult female survivors. *Alcoholism Treatment Quarterly*, **7**, 41–56.

Ireland, T. and Widom, C.S. (1994). Childhood victimisation and risk for alcoholism and drug arrests. *International Journal of Addiction*, **29**, 235–74.

Khantzian, E.J. (1985). The self-medication hypothesis of addictive behaviours: focus on heroin and cocaine dependence. *American Journal of Psychiatry*, **142**, 1259–64.

Martin, C.R. and Hewitt, G. (1996). Alcohol, memory and cognition. In Bonner, A.B. and Waterhouse, J. (eds), *Addictive Behaviour: Molecules to Mankind*, pp. 135–57. London: Macmillan.

Martin, C.R. and Otter, C.R. (1996). Locus of control and addictive behaviour. In Bonner, A.B. and Waterhouse, J. (eds), *Addictive Behaviour: Molecules to Mankind*, pp. 121–34. London: Macmillan.

Mash, M.R., Hulsey, T.L., Sexton, M.C., Harralson, T.L. and Lambert, W. (1993). Long-term sequelae of childhood sexual abuse: perceived family environment, psychopathology, and dissociation. *Journal of Consulting Clinical Psychology*, **61**, 276–83.

Mullen, P.E., Martin, J.L., Anderson, J.C., Romans, S.E. and Herbison, G.P. (1993). Childhood sexual abuse and mental health in adult life. *British Journal of Psychiatry*, **163**, 721–32.

Orford, J. and Harwin, J. (1982). *Alcohol and the Family*. London: Croom Helm.

Tajfel, H. (1982). *Social Identity and Intergroup Relations*. Cambridge: Cambridge University Press.

CHAPTER 5

Young people and drug use: an analysis of motivation and experience – the lessons for policy makers and practitioners

David Best

In the government White Paper *Tackling Drugs Together* (1995) the objectives set out for young people for 1995 to 1998 include minimizing the proportion of young people who experiment with drugs and encouraging 'youth services and other agencies in contact with young people to play a part in alerting them to the dangers of drugs, and advising those who may already be experimenting of the services available to help them stop' (White Paper *Together* 1995, p. 17). On the other hand, the Task Force to Review Services for Drug Misusers (1996) argues that meeting the needs of young drug misusers is likely to involve 'drug services specifically dedicated to young people' (p. 22).

Policy makers are caught in an awkward situation in which primary prevention represents the ideal, yet the use of harm reduction approaches, relatively successful with adult substance misusers, may be a more realistic approach for young people who may already be using substantial quantities of both licit and illicit drugs. The goal of this chapter will be to examine the evidence concerning the extent and severity of substance use among young people in the context of their own perceptions and experiences, and to use this participative strategy in suggesting appropriate steps forward for drugs educators and policy makers.

EXISTING EVIDENCE

The most recent *British Crime Survey* (Ramsey and Percey 1996) suggests that 43 per cent of 16- to 29-year-olds have tried an illicit substance, with the most commonly used illicit drug being cannabis. Similarly, Miller and Plant's (1996) school-based study of 7,722 students between the ages of 15 and 16 years shows that 42.3 per cent report having used an illicit drug. Furthermore, the authors also demonstrate marked regional variability, with, for example, 59.9 per cent of Scottish boys reporting having used an illicit drug compared with only 35.0 per cent of the Welsh boys sampled. The data from these two studies exceed Parker *et al.*'s (1995) findings, only a year earlier, that the prevalence of illicit drug use among 15- to 20-year-olds is between 10 and 35 per cent in national surveys.

The data on prevalence is supported by trend estimates which suggest significant increases in both licit and illicit substance use by young people in recent years. Balding (1994) has argued that 15- and 16-year-olds' use of cannabis leaf has trebled between 1989 and 1993, and that the use of amphetamines and solvents by this age group has also increased in the same period. Balding has also argued that 'by 1995 half of all 15–16 year old boys in the United Kingdom may have experimented with cannabis, and over 80 per cent of young people in this age group will report that they know at least one person that takes drugs' (Balding 1994). The suggestion that the accessibility of drugs to young people is increasing, in addition to the active use, is supported by Wright and Pearl's (1995) evidence from a twenty-five-year cross-sectional study that 14- and 15-year-olds' exposure to illicit substances has significantly increased between 1969 and 1994.

The evidence of high and increasing levels of access to and uptake of substances is not confined to illicit substances, with similar evidence existing for both tobacco and alcohol. The Miller and Plant (1996) school study shows that 67.6 per cent of their total sample of 15- and 16-year-olds had at some time smoked cigarettes and that only 5.8 per cent reported that they had never consumed alcohol. Furthermore, 77.9 per cent reported that they had experienced alcoholic intoxication at some point, of whom 48.3 per cent had been intoxicated in the past thirty days. This evidence is supported by the *Drug Misuse in Britain* (ISDD 1994) report, which claims that males of 16 years and over drink an average of one and a half pints of beer a day and that, by the age of 16 to 17, 23 per cent of males and 20 per cent of females regularly smoke cigarettes.

INTERPRETING PREVALENCE ESTIMATES

The findings presented above are of particular concern to parents, teachers and politicians alike as it has been argued that drunkenness and illicit drug use before the age of 15 is predictive of adult substance use, especially at more severe levels (Robins and Przybeck 1985; Robins and McEvoy 1990). However, evidence for the 'gateway theory' – that early use of substances such as cannabis and alcohol are predictive of adult substance problems – is far from clear and often based on retrospective recall of adult substance users (Bukstein 1995). The problems in interpreting the many prevalence studies that have been carried out are twofold – the first concerns the accuracy of the information presented and the second its value in attempting to develop interventions and policy.

The debate about accuracy of self-reported substance use is not restricted to young people and has provoked a number of methodological investigations in the field of adult research and intervention that are worthy of mention. Davies and Best (1996) have argued that the use of forced-choice questionnaires enhances the demand characteristics inherent in all question–answer formats (for example, the desire of the respondent to appear intelligent and attractive) and so influence the responses to both attitudinal and behavioural items. Davies (1996) has continued this theme by arguing that self-report is 'likely to reflect the context in which the account is obtained and the motives of the person involved rather than any direct "scientific" account of "fact" or "truth"'. In an earlier study Davies and Baker (1988) found that when addicts were interviewed by a formal interviewer in a suit they reported higher levels of substance use, lower levels of control and greater addiction than when interviewed by someone they knew to be a fellow user.

These methodological concerns about self-report are reflected in the literature concerning adolescent substance activity. Winters (1990) claims that certain populations of young people are more likely to provide false socially desirable responses than are adult substance users. Such reports have led to Bukstein's (1995) conclusion that the extent and frequency of drug use among young people has been greatly exaggerated. The problem is that, while some young people may feel that it is socially desirable to exaggerate their substance experience (that it may be 'grown up' or 'tough'), others may underestimate for fear of punishment. The variations reported by Parker, Measham and Aldridge (1995), in their meta-analysis of the existing literature (10 to 35 per cent in national samples and 5 to 50 per cent in local samples in populations of 15- to 20-year-olds) provide further evidence of the confusing epidemiological base on which policy makers are expected to develop strategies and interventions.

The emphasis that has been placed on prevalence of illicit substance activity may be unnecessary as well as being inconsistent and of dubious methodological worth. While there may be certain benefits in assessing the frequency of substance activity in young people and the amounts consumed, this data in isolation is not especially helpful. Quantity–frequency indices provide only a baseline against which patterns of substance use, problems encountered and reasons for use may be examined. Prevalence results have not been shown to be reliable and should be treated with care with regard to policy implications. Theories that young people use drugs because they do not know enough about the negative consequences or because they are victims of an insidious peer pressure, are assumptions the validity of which, does not appear consistent with current evidence. Indeed, Best and Barrie (1996) found that many young people make considered judgements based on personal experience and group debates (rather than pressures) when making choices that relate to their use of both licit and illicit drugs.

YOUNG PEOPLE'S EXPLANATIONS FOR SUBSTANCE ACTIVITY

Two concerns frequently voiced concerning adolescent substance use involve predicting adult behaviour from adolescent activity, and the immediate problems for the young user and for those with whom he or she has contact. As indicated, evidence on the predictive power of adolescent substance activity is weak. Kandel and Logan (1984) argue that marijuana use peaks in late adolescence and then begins to decline, and that patterns of use of other illicit drugs follow a similar pattern. An equivalent claim has been advanced about adolescent alcohol use by Blane (1976), who found that heavy drinking in adolescence and its resultant problems are not predictive of alcoholism in adults.

It is not surprising, however, that the evidence on the long-term predictive capabilities of adolescent substance activities are limited as the time gap between the adolescent behaviour and the adult outcome is so great, and so there is scope for any number of intervening, confounding variables. As a consequence, it is the number of risk factors (such as poor socioeconomic status, poor housing or high population density) that predicts adult substance activity better than any individual risk factor, such as adolescent drug or alcohol activity. Therefore it is the argument concerning the immediate detrimental effects of alcohol or illicit drug use that may be of greater relevance (as well as scientific decidability).

The focus of the remainder of this chapter will be on what young people think of drugs and why they use or may use them, and to explore the implications that these issues may have for policy and education. Coffield and Gofton (1994) concluded their investigation of young people's drug use by suggesting that drug use is not problematic to young people who believe they can control what they regard as 'soft' drugs, and they also claimed that it is alcohol and tobacco use that creates greater problems for young people. Similarly, Hirst and McCamley-Finney (1994) challenged the idea that illicit substance activity is a central life focus for young people who are using. Indeed, they argue that 'young people are aware of the presence of drugs in their social worlds and, in the main, they treat this matter of factly and find ways of coping with, or responding to it as a matter of course'.

This claim, suggesting that the dramatic outpourings of politicians and the popular press may not be reflected in the attitudes or activities of young people, is supported by Davies and Coggans (1991). They claim that it is the social context of illicit drug use that causes the greatest difficulty for young people, rather than the unlikely outcomes of addiction or dependence. This is reflected in the infrequency with which young people attempt to contact addiction services or present to health services with substance-related problems. Best and Barrie (1996) reported that many young people contrast their 'safe' use of 'happy' drugs such as ecstasy and LSD with what they perceive as the 'junkie' drugs of heroin and cocaine, which they were convinced that they would never use. Although there may be a self-selection bias, with young people unlikely to identify their substance use as problematic, it is very unusual for young substance users to satisfy the criteria for abuse or dependence stated in the diagnostic manual for psychiatric assessment (DSM-IV, Bukstein 1995).

However, it is precisely the perceptions of the target population that are required to increase the accuracy of targeting and applicability of interventions. In Best and Barrie's (1996) investigation of young people's substance activity in the Easterhouse area of Glasgow, a questionnaire was completed by and designed on the basis of almost 150 informal interviews carried out with young people in the area in an attempt to conduct a research project based on the perceptions of those taking part and the issues of concern to them. In the study 12- to 19-year-olds reported levels of substance use in excess of the figures reported by Miller and Plant (1996), with questionnaire respondents reporting lifetime prevalence for cannabis of 5 cent, for LSD of 35.5 per cent and for temazepam of 33.9 per cent. It is interesting to note, however, that the equivalent figures for current use are 36.6 per cent for cannabis, 13.4 per cent for LSD and 17.2 per cent for temazepam. This group would appear to fulfil all of Brook and Brook's (1990) criteria of low socioeconomic status, high population density, physical deterioration and low population mobility for high levels of adolescent substance abuse.

However, the stories that the young people themselves tell of their substance activities, although high in prevalence and quantity of use, are of controlled and intentional substance use. For many of the young people in the study illicit drugs were perceived as a positive, recreational aspect of their lives and it was common for them to be puzzled by the suggestion that their drug use was problematic or dangerous. It also became apparent that the young people were well aware of the risks associated with drug use but that they did not feel that these risks applied to their own patterns of substance activity. It was particularly common for young people to contrast their own use of 'happy' and 'soft' drugs with the use of 'bad' drugs such as heroin and cocaine which are regarded as the domain of drug problems and addiction.

IMPLICATIONS FOR INTERVENTIONS AND DRUG EDUCATION

Blackman (1996) found that, while young people reported that they wanted more drug education, they often reported that what they were receiving was too negative and inconsistent with their own experiences and knowledge of drugs. Similarly, the 1992 *British Crime Survey* (Dowds and Redfern, 1994) found that young people who had tried drugs were more likely to seek information from friends than from teachers or parents. This is compounded by Wright and Pearl's (1995) finding that television is the main source of young people's drugs awareness. Coggans *et al.* (1991) also argue that, although drugs education would appear to have a positive impact on drugs knowledge, the majority of research shows that drugs knowledge among young people is relatively poor. This is particularly problematic, as O'Connor (1995) points out, in that very little is known about the quantity or quality of drugs education provision in Britain.

Much of this evidence is supported in Best and Barrie's (1996) Easterhouse study, in which the most common source of information about drugs was friends, who were also reported as the group respondents would turn to if they had a drug problem. The young people in the study favoured using ex-users or drug workers as educators and most did not believe that teachers were the most suitable providers of drugs education. However, the study also demonstrated differences in attitudes to drugs education according to the respondents' own levels of substance involvement. Those who report highest levels of satisfaction with drugs education in schools are also those who have experimented with and are currently using the fewest illicit substances. It was also found that participants who felt teachers were not suitable providers of drugs education had significantly higher levels of lifetime and current substance activity than those who felt the reverse. The suggestion that young people's attitudes to drugs education may vary as a function of their own drug experiences would appear to have significant implications for designing interventions.

The first point to make here is that young people are not short of potential sources of information for drugs education – however accurate or inaccurate, drug information is readily available in newspapers and on television, as well as from friends, siblings, teachers and parents. Therefore for a school-based intervention to make a significant impact it must be of sufficient relevance and salience to its target audience that it can successfully compete with other potential information sources. As Best et al. (1995) found in their evaluation of a project designing and developing a drugs information booklet for young people, materials must be 'informative, relevant, not too literature-based, in a language familiar to young people and amusing'. Conversely, it is likely that successful interventions will avoid moral or didactic styles and will attempt to engage the young people in a challenging, interactive process.

For this reason it would appear crucial that, prior to the introduction of any drugs education intervention, the levels of awareness and activity, as well as the drugs and drugs-education-related attitudes, of the young people should be assessed. It is not that the use of abstinence-oriented or information-based packages are universally inappropriate but that their suitability is contingent upon the experiences and perceptions of the target audience. However, the requirement to match the intervention to the target population is indicative of a general shift from monologue to dialogue that is likely to characterize more meaningful school-based drugs-related interactions for young people.

Evaluations of drugs education such as those carried out by Schaps et al. (1981) and by Kinder, Pape and Walfish (1980) have concluded that drugs education measures are largely ineffective in influencing substance activity. This is because what is required is not education in the sense of distributing knowledge. It is also unreasonable to attempt to educate a group whose existing level of knowledge is unassessed – where should the lessons be pitched, and how do we know what the young people's strengths and weaknesses are?

What is required for the many young people for whom 'the use of illegal drugs ... has become normalised' (Paraskeva, 1995) is a forum in which they can discuss and make sense of their drug experiences, and from which relevant information, advice and support may be provided. It is only by including the young people whose well-being is central to the process of drugs education that it may be possible to develop a strategy that makes sense for them and so has a realistic prospect of altering their substance-related behaviour, whether in the direction of abstinence or, as Cohen (1992) suggests, in the implementation of an approach based on harm reduction.

The key is that the philosophy adopted is of only limited value, and probably ineffective, if it is not compatible with the needs of the young people who represent its critical outcome. As Best and Barrie (1996) found, it is not that young people need more information on 'legal issues' or 'side effects', it is that they need to be involved to a greater extent in all aspects and stages of the drugs education process. For interventions to have the necessary impact, they must engage the young people, and this requires their active participation.

Finally, for policy makers and educators in this area, it is critical that this participative approach, based on the involvement of young people, should be

sustained by a reflective and critical evaluation policy. The
sufficient merely to design yet another drug education pack,
reduction or any other philosophy, and think that this is
interventions must be carefully evaluated both in process and
and those evaluative variables that relate to outcome must be
beneficial to in behavioural terms for the young people and the teachers
involved in this collaborative process.

CONCLUSION

The recognition of both the availability of licit and illicit drugs to young
people and the consequent increase in their uptake has alerted policy makers
and educators alike to the need for an effective response. However, the year-
ly increases in prevalence indices are accompanied by growing fears that
existing interventions may be ineffective or even counter-productive. As a
consequence it is important that changes should be made in the design of
interventions to involve and stimulate their target audiences without alienating moral and social assumptions, and that projects should be evaluated in
terms of clearly defined goals and the outcome of monitoring strategies.

REFERENCES

Balding, J. (1994) *Young People and Illegal Drugs, 1989–1995*. Exeter: University of Exeter Schools Health Education Unit.

Best, D. and Barrie, A. (1996) *Substance Activity and Attitudes among 12 to
19 Year Olds in Greater Easterhouse: A Participative Outreach Resarch
Study*. Glasgow: Easterhouse Drugs Initiative.

Best, D., Mortimer, R. and Davies, J. (1995) *Evaluation of the Fast Forward
Peer Research Project*. Report to Fast Forward Positive Lifestyles Ltd.

Blackman, S. (1996) *Drugs Education and the National Curriculum: An
Evaluation of drug studies*. Resources for the National Curriculum, vol. 11,
Drugs Prevention Initiative. London: HMSO.

Blane, H.T. (1976) Sex of siblings of male alcoholics. *Archives of General
Psychiatry*, **32**(11), 1403–5.

Brook, D. and Brook, J. (1990) The etiology and consequences of drug use. In
Watson, R. (ed.) *Drug and Alcohol Abuse Prevention*. Clifton, NJ: Humana
Press, pp. 339–62.

Bukstein, O.G. (1995) *Adolescent Substance Abuse: Assessment, Prevention
and Treatment*. New York: John Wiley and Sons Inc.

Coffield, F. and Gofton, L. (1994) *Drugs and Young People*. London: Institute
for Public Policy Research.

Coggans, N.D., Shewan, D., Henderson, M., Davies, J.B. and O'Hagen, F.J.
(1991), *National Evaluation of Drug Education in Scotland: Final Report*.
Edinburgh: Scottish Education Department.

Cohen, J. (1992) Achieving a reduction in drug-related harm through educa-
tion. In Heather, N., Wodak, A., Nadelmann, E. and O'Hare, P. (eds),
Psychoactive Drugs and Harm Reduction: From Faith to Service. London:
Whurr.

Davies, J.B. (1996) Conversations with drug users: a functional discourse
model. *Addiction Research*, **5**(1), 1–18.

ies, J.B. and Baker, S. (1988) The impact of self presentation and interviewer bias effects on self reported heroin use. *British Journal of Addiction*, **82**, 907–12.

Davies, J.B. and Best, D.W. (1996) Demand characteristics and research into drug use. *Psychology and Health*, **11**, 291–99.

Davies, J.B. and Coggans, N. (1991) *The Facts about Adolescent Drug Use*. London: Cassell.

Dowds, L. and Redfern, J. (1994) *Drug Education amongst Teenagers: A 1992 British Crime Survey Analysis*. Research and Planning Unit, Paper 86. London: HMSO.

Hirst, J. and McCamley-Finney, F. (1994) *The Place and Meaning of Drugs in the Lives of Young People*. Health Research Institute Report No. 7. Sheffield: Hallam University.

Institute for the Study of Drug Dependence (1994) *Drug Misuse in Britain in 1994*. London: ISDD.

Kandel, D. and Logan, J. (1984) Patterns of drug use from adolescence to young adulthood. *American Journal of Public Health*, **74**, 660–6.

Kinder, B.N., Pape, N.E. and Walfish, S. (1980), Drug and alcohol education programmes: a review of outcome studies. *International Journal of Addiction*, **15**, 1035–54.

Miller, P. and Plant, M. (1996) Drinking, smoking and illicit drug use among 15 and 16 year olds in the United Kingdom. *British Medical Journal*, **313**, 394–7.

O'Connor, L. (1995) Drug education in schools: getting it right. Paper presented to the London Drugs Policy Forum Conference, 24 March 1995, *Youth Culture – Drug Culture*. London: Drugs Policy Forum.

Paraskeva, J. (1995) Paper presented to the London Drugs Policy Forum Conference, 24 March 1995, *Youth Culture – Drug Culture*. London: Drugs Policy Forum.

Parker, H., Measham, F. and Aldridge, J. (1995) *Drug Futures: Changing Patterns of Drug Use amongst English Youth*. ISDD Monograph Research No. 7. London: ISDD.

Ramsey, M. and Percey, A. (1996) *Drug Misuse Declared: Results of the 1994 British Crime Survey*. Research Findings No. 36, London: HMSO.

Robins, L. and McEvoy, L. (1990) Conduct problems as predictors of substance abuse. In Robins, L.N. and Rutter, M. (eds), *Straight and Devious Pathways from Childhood to Adulthood*, pp. 182–204. Cambridge: Cambridge University Press.

Robins, L. and Przybeck, T. (1985) Age of onset of drug use as a risk factor in drug and other disorders. In Jones, C.L. and Battjes, R.J. (eds), *Implications for Prevention*, pp. 178–92. Rockville, MD: National Institute for Drug Abuse, Department of Health and Human Services.

Schaps, E., Bartolo, R., Moskowitz, J.M., Palley, C. and Chugrin, S. (1981) A review of 127 drug abuse prevention program initiatives. *Journal of Drug Issues*, **11**, 17–24.

Task Force to Review Services for Drug Misusers (1996) *Report of an Independent Review of Drug Treatment Services in England*. London: Department of Health.

White Paper (1995) *Tackling Drugs Together: A Strategy for England, 1995–1998.* CMD 2846. London: HMSO.

Winters, K. (1990) The need for improved assessment of adolescent substance involvement. *Journal of Drug Issues,* **20**, 487–502.

Wright, J. and Pearl, L. (1995) Knowledge and experience of young people regarding drug misuse, 1969–1994. *British Medical Journal,* **309**, 20–4.

PART 2

Drugs Education: Context, Consensus and Communication

CHAPTER 6

What 'works' in drugs education?

Louise O'Connor, David Best and Rachel Best

INTRODUCTION

The variability in the provision of drugs education in schools is linked not only to resource difficulties but to the problems for schools in identifying and accessing approaches which are most likely to succeed. These problems are compounded by differing interpretations of 'effectiveness'. The aims of drugs education in schools are rarely clarified, for example, is success to be measured in terms of preventing drug use altogether, persuading drug users to stop, or reducing harm to those resistant to cessation exhortations? (We use the term 'drugs' to include the range of legal and illegal substances available in varying degrees to young people.)

The purpose of this chapter is to review approaches to drugs education in the context of a critical evaluation of their effectiveness, and to identify key principles to inform school drugs education. To achieve this, the chapter will draw on lessons from the literature and first-hand research conducted in three London boroughs amongst nearly 4,500 young people aged 5 to 18.

THE LITERATURE: APPROACHES TO DRUGS EDUCATION – AN OVERVIEW

Since 1988 drugs education has been a statutory requirement of the Science Curriculum in primary and secondary schools. The government White Paper *Tackling Drugs Together* (1995) further requires schools to develop policies for managing drug-related incidents and education programmes. The framework for policy development is provided in guidance documents Circular 4/95 *Drug Prevention and Schools* (DfE 1995) and *Drug Education: Curriculum Guidance for Schools* (SCAA/DfE 1995). However, both the quality and quantity of drugs education in schools varies widely, apparently depending on individual school commitment and expertise (Ofsted 1997). O'Connor (1991), in a case study of a middle school implementing a health education programme, ascertained that teacher confidence and expertise were crucial factors in addressing sensitive areas of the health curriculum; drugs education was either ignored or covered inappropriately by teachers lacking both.

edge, understanding and capability also feature in other studies
problems of curriculum implementation around drugs issues

ns in implementation identified from the literature, there have
a number of approaches to drugs education in the UK, which have been
used either singly or in a variety of combinations. These have been based
loosely on the following:

- deterrence approaches, including 'scare tactics' and 'just say no' exhortations;
- factual or informational education, which aims to give unbiased, accurate information about drugs and drugs issues;
- affective or self-empowerment education, which aims to boost self-
  esteem, assertiveness and decision-making skills, and increase belief in
  personal interest and control;
- situational education, which acknowledges the social context of, and
  influences on, personal choices around drug taking; and
- the cultural approach, which favours a broader context of the life skills
  teaching, acknowledging the influence of homes, communities and work
  on lifestyles and behaviour.

(Health Advisory Service 1996; O'Connor 1995)

The most common form of drugs education in Britain has been based on a
primary prevention model in which the objective is the promotion of a drug-
free lifestyle. However, the effectiveness of the abstinence approach has been
questioned, with several studies challenging its long-term ability to influence
behaviour (Swadi 1988; Kinder, Pape and Walfish 1980). In a meta-analysis of
drugs education programmes, Wragg (1992) concluded that a combination of
all the above approaches (excluding scare tactics and the 'just say no' method)
was most likely to succeed in terms of impacting on knowledge and behaviour.

A similar problem has arisen with the content as well as the philosophy of
drugs education interventions, with Kinder, Pape and Walfish (1980) also
arguing that certain programmes based solely on drug information techniques
may actually increase drug use among young people. This finding challenges
the assumption on which drugs education has traditionally been founded,
namely that young people use drugs because they lack sufficient information
about their effects. That young people use drugs as a result of peer pressure
has also been challenged in recent years (Health Advisory Service 1996).
These problems concerning both the philosophy and the content of school-
based drugs education are compounded by O'Connor's (1995) finding that
'despite the fact that drugs education has been a compulsory element of the
Science National Curriculum since 1988, little is known about the overall
quantity and quality of provision'. Further evidence has arisen out of the
Ofsted monitoring exercise of drugs policies in schools. Whilst some good
practice has been identified, a lack of coherent planning, clear aims and
objectives and evaluation results in patchy, piecemeal provision (Ofsted
1997).

The Health Advisory Service (1996) has argued that drugs education in
schools has not only been overly influenced by the alleged contribution of

peer pressure and self-esteem in causing drug use, but has also failed to account for the range of ages and social backgrounds of the target audience and has viewed substance use too much in isolation, rather than as one aspect of problem behaviour. Thus, whilst the Health Education Authority (1992) has shown that 90 per cent of schools held health education programmes in which drugs learning may have occurred, the research evidence is not supportive of its efficacy, to the limited extent that research and evaluation have occurred. This is to some extent substantiated by surveys conducted with young people. For example, the 1992 *British Crime Survey* found that only 44 per cent of 12- to 15-year-olds were certain that they had ever received drugs education lessons, while only one-third of the sample had received a drugs education lesson in the last six to eight months (Dowds and Redfern 1994). Given meta-analysis findings that long-term, sustained education programmes hold out most chance of success, these findings are not positive indicators of wide-spread effective provision in schools. Further cause for concern is justified by the Ofsted findings (1997) that, whilst over 60 per cent of observed lessons were rated 'good' and a further 25 per cent 'satisfactory', 'too many schools fail to make an *assessment* of pupils' knowledge and understanding of drugs before planning and teaching the programme'. This situation is further com-pounded by lack of attempts to measure changes in knowledge, skills or understanding through monitoring and evaluation.

However, there is evidence that young people generally value drugs educa-tion, although this is least likely to be the case with those who have already experienced illicit drugs (Dowds and Redfern 1994). Ofsted (1997) exem-plifies the conditions in which learning about drugs is most likely to be a positive experience as when 'The teacher established a setting in which the pupils were able to talk confidently about their understanding of the issues surrounding drug use and misuse. The establishment of a code of conduct in such lessons was a key feature in the success of much of this work'. Similarly, Coggans *et al.* (1991) found that some drugs education does appear to have a positive impact on drugs knowledge, while the Kent County Constabulary (1995) report found that young people wanted to know about the effects of drugs and what are safe and unsafe drugs. Blackman (1996) also reported that young people were generally very positive about the concept of drugs educa-tion, although most wanted it tailored to their needs more accurately. In their evaluation of the Youth Awareness Programme, Shiner and Newburn (1996) rejected the idea that young people were unwilling to listen to adults, but stressed that the educator must have credibility in the area of substance awareness or activity.

A second source of optimism derives from the willingness of educators to learn from the mistakes of the past and to accept the recommendations for a more sophisticated and interactive framework within which drugs education may increase its effectiveness. Thus, Coggans and Watson (1995) have sug-gested that multi-media and multi-strand interventions are more likely to be effective than interventions that rely on one single approach. These initiatives have included peer education programmes in which those with recent experi-ence of an active drug culture may be used as educators, and community action programmes in which, for example, a health-promoting school approach is used, are currently being implemented and evaluated. O'Connor's work with sixth-formers (1995) also led her to suggest that drugs education needs to be related to young people's perceptions of drug issues and their needs, that the deliverers be suitably skilled and trained and that drugs education be located within a wider context of promoting healthy behaviour.

Thus, the foundations of drugs education have been challenged in terms of both their assumptions about the causes of drug-using behaviour and the objectives of their procedures. The problems would appear to be that few outcome studies have been carried out assessing the effectiveness of drugs education in terms of knowledge gain, attitude and behaviour change, and those that exist do not always provide much encouragement for practitioners. However, some approaches, notably peer education, indicate some short-term changes in behaviour relating to harm reduction (Shiner and Newburn 1996). In the longer term, Stead *et al.* (1996) illustrate, through a comprehensive review of adolescent smoking prevention programmes, the unrealistic expectations of short-term, single-stranded education interventions. The authors conclude that sustained, multi-faceted approaches hold out the best chance of success, particularly if social policy measures back educational and community efforts.

Research has revealed that the credibility of drugs educators is of major importance. O'Connor (1995) discovered that young people were not over-concerned about the profession of the educator yet they perceived the credibility – good knowledge of drugs, good teaching skills, open-mindedness and empathy for the audience – to be paramount. However, Blackman (1996) found that teachers tended to have negative perceptions of their own ability to teach drugs education and were uncertain of the location of drugs education in the National Curriculum. Noble (1996) argued that the attitude of the teaching staff and the head teacher is critical in establishing the ethos of the school, and that the happiness of the teaching staff is likely to be reflected in the quality of their teaching. Teachers lacking in confidence in their ability to teach drugs education are likely to lack commitment and conviction. (See also O'Connor 1991.) Ofsted (1997) found that the weakest teaching of drugs education lessons generally occurred in Key Stage 3, within tutorial lessons. This has implications for the preferred location of drugs lessons, and the training and support given to key deliverers.

The DfE Circular 4/95 *Drug Prevention and Schools* guidance document recommends that the use of outside speakers, in the form of multi-agency contributions, to school drugs education can have a positive impact on the quality of drugs education. However, it is also recommended that outside inputs should be part of a co-ordinated drugs education programme organized by the school as opposed to being an opportunity for schools to pass the responsibility of drugs education on to an external body. Although multi-agency networks seem a good idea in principle, Sidebottom (1995) found that inputs tended to occur on an *ad hoc* basis and Canavan (1995) discovered that mixed messages occurred in the teaching of drugs education since speakers failed to communicate with each other prior to teaching. Ofsted (1997) also states that this is a problem if programmes are not carefully planned and co-ordinated.

On a wider front the community has an important role to play with regard to young people and drugs. For example, shopkeepers have a duty to ensure that illegal alcohol and tobacco sales are not made to under-age young people; residents' associations can work with police and local authorities to remove illegal drug dealing from residential areas (O'Connor 1992). The Central Drug Co-ordination Unit (CDCU) has produced *A Practical Guide for Drug Action Teams* (1996) which documents examples of well-planned community initiatives capable of reducing incidents of drug misuse, provided they are informed by views from the community.

A collaborative research project conducted by Roehampton Institute London with Merton, Sutton and Wandsworth Health Authority provides further illumination on approaches to drugs education most likely to be 'effective' at least in matching the perceptions, experiences and expressed needs of young people.

RESEARCH PROJECT

The research project conducted by O'Connor *et al.* (1997) used a relatively large sample of young people (approximately 4,500) within a comparatively small geographical area (the London boroughs of Merton, Sutton and Wandsworth). The study was designed to investigate young people's understanding, perceptions, experience and attitudes regarding drugs and drugs education. The investigation used a multiple methodology to develop a set of policy implications and recommendations with regard to drugs education. A brief overview of the methods and main findings and implications is given below.

A COLLABORATIVE RESEARCH PROJECT IN THREE LONDON BOROUGHS

Focus on the 'Draw and Write' study

A total of 1,941 primary school children aged 4 to 11 completed a 'draw and write' task produced by Williams *et al.* (1989). Of the sample 49 per cent were female and 40 per cent were male (the remaining 11 per cent failed to indicate their gender). Pupils were asked a series of questions about a story in which a young child finds a bag of 'drugs' in a park in an attempt to identify the extent of their awareness about drugs. Thirty-four special needs children aged 11–16 also completed the 'draw and write' task.

Findings and implications

The most common reply to the question 'What do you think was in the bag?' was tablets and medicines, reported by 33.6 per cent of the primary school children and by 50 per cent of the special needs children. However, the findings imply that National Curriculum science teaching on the use of drugs as medicines is not particularly well received by Key Stage 1 pupils, since only 23 per cent of 4- to 6-year-olds compared with 43 per cent of 10- to 11-year-olds labelled drugs as medicines. Whilst there were no gender differences in the reporting of specific responses, clear age effects were demonstrated, with 4- to 7-year-olds appearing to have limited understanding of the concept of drugs. Age effects were also demonstrated in that a number of 10- and 11-year-olds appear to have a reasonably sophisticated understanding of a range of drugs issues, whilst the special needs children exhibit a level of awareness similar to that of the older primary school children aged 10 to 11.

The results would suggest that beyond the age of 7 years young people have a conception of drugs although this may often be imprecise and flawed. For instance, when asked what they would have done if they found the bag, the answers included 'make sweets out of it', 'eat it' and 'take it to the bank'. The notion of 'drug dealing' also appears to emerge at around 7 years. The depiction of a range of male stereotypes as the person who lost the bag in the story (females were very rarely mentioned) indicates that primary school children have an unrealistic perception of drug users as 'mad, bad and sad'. The secondary schools research shows this is a dangerous misperception on behalf of primary school pupils (see below). Therefore, it is important that teachers have an understanding of their pupils' drugs awareness so they can create an appropriate starting point for drugs education. Information and approaches need to be carefully geared to pupils level of drugs knowledge, perceptions, understanding and misunderstanding.

The findings further indicate that the belief that drugs 'are bad for you' also develops with age, from 37 per cent of 4- to 6-year-olds, to 93 per cent of 10- to 11-year-olds. This unbalanced view of drugs in general may come from depictions of illegal drugs and illegal activity through sensationalist reporting on television and fictional drama. The researchers and teachers involved had no reason to believe that, except in a small minority of cases, the sampled children had first-hand experience of illicit drugs. On the other hand, 26 per cent of 4- to 5-year-olds, rising to 42 per cent of 10- to 11-year-olds, had televisions in their bedrooms. Previous research has suggested that television is a prime source of knowledge about drugs for primary school children (Williams, Wetton and Moon 1989). Sources of drugs information should be of concern to parents as well as teachers. Children substitute their own 'sense' for information not understood. If these substitutions are not acknowledged by teachers, further misunderstandings can result (Wetton 1992). In particular, children need some strategies for refusing unknown substances from friends and acquaintances. The research indicates that they believe drugs come from 'dealers' or other unknown adults. The reality gleaned from the secondary school research is that friends and acquaintances are most likely to offer drugs.

Primary schools have a history of involving parents in all kinds of curriculum initiatives, and home–school relations are a particular priority. The sensitive nature of drugs issues present a particular challenge to primary schools, but given their commitment to partnerships with parents, opportunities to tackle the issues can be found and utilized to good effect. One primary school, with a particular commitment to health education, had involved governors and parents in identifying the problems which needed addressing. (See also Ofsted 1997.)

SECONDARY SCHOOL RESEARCH

Part One: Questionnaire study and group discussion study

A questionnaire was distributed to 2,440 secondary school pupils aged 10 to 18. Of the sample 76 per cent were female while 18 per cent were male (the remaining 6 per cent failed to indicate their gender). The majority of respondents described their ethnic status as white (71 per cent). The imbalance in gender sampling was due to the 'opportunity' basis of the questionnaire distribution. Overall, girls' schools were keener to participate than boys' schools.

Six group discussions were conducted with a number of pupils who completed the questionnaire, although two of the groups were involved in two sets of discussions as part of a reflexive methodology – in their initial discussion they discussed general drugs issues, while the follow-up topics revolved around drugs education.

Part Two: Secondary school pupils' experiences of drugs and drugs education

In the questionnaire 2,122 (87 per cent) claimed to have tried alcohol, 1,310 (54 per cent) claimed to have tried tobacco and 416 (17 per cent) claimed to have tried an illicit drug in their lifetime. In general, these levels of substance activity are in line with findings from national surveys on the prevalence of drugs use (ISDD 1994; HEA 1992). There was a correlation between dependent smokers (126 = 5 per cent) and illicit drug use. The latter group were approximately twenty-two times more likely to have tried illicit drugs. Frequent alcohol and tobacco use were also independently correlated with illegal drugs use. That is, participants who reported drinking or smoking on a 'regular' basis were more likely to have tried an illicit drug.

The majority of young people (70 per cent) claimed they had received drugs education many or a few times. Of those who reported having received drugs education, 478 (24 per cent) reported that they found it 'very useful', 1,204 (62 per cent) that they found it 'fairly useful' and only 249 (13 per cent) that they found it 'not at all useful'. The latter group were generally drawn from those young people who had experienced legal and illegal drugs (see below). It is also interesting to note that 1,760 (72 per cent) thought it 'very important' that young people should be taught about drugs while only 11 (0.5 per cent) thought that it was 'not at all important'. The group discussions also revealed that young people were keen to learn about drugs issues but considered the quality of the education could be better. It is also significant to note that realism was frequently quoted as a key ingredient, with support for involving ex-users partly a means of avoiding what many young people perceive as the propagandist approach in schools. The key requirement for drugs educators focused on their perceived 'knowledge' on drugs and drugs issues.

When asked what they would like to know about drugs in the questionnaire, the most common responses were 'the effects of drugs' (51 per cent), the 'street names' for drugs (45 per cent), 'drug appearances' (53 per cent) and 'where to go for help' (42 per cent). With regard to the deliverer of drugs information, the most favoured of the options provided was 'ex-user' selected by 61 per cent, followed by 'parents' (53 per cent), 'drug counsellor' (52 per cent) then 'books or magazines' (51 per cent). In both sets of group discussions one of the most powerful themes was the belief in ex-users as drug educators. Many of the young people felt that ex-users were well equipped to give first-hand accounts, while the suitability of teachers was undermined as they 'don't know what they are talking about' and, because they know the young people, it is impossible to be open in front of them. This preference for anonymity may explain the popularity that was reported in the questionnaire phase of the study of phone lines as supports for drug problems.

Those who reported having used an illicit drug in the questionnaire reported different attitudes to drugs education to those who did not report any drug experiences. Whilst 11 per cent of the total sample said they would speak to their drugs education teacher if they had a drug problem, this was the case for only 6 per cent of those who use illicit drugs regularly (defined as 'at least once a month', n = 158). Similarly, 22 per cent of this regular drug use group did not find drugs education to be useful at all, compared to 13 per cent of the total sample. Finally, while 49 per cent of the regular user group reported that they could learn from current users (compared to 30 per cent of the total sample), only 32 per cent of the regular users report that they could learn something from their health education teacher at school, compared with 46 per cent of the total group. Therefore, while the results for the whole group may be encouraging from the perspective of drug educators, this is mediated by the young persons' own experience of illicit drugs.

IMPLICATION FOR SCHOOLS, PARENTS AND COMMUNITIES OF DRUGS AND DRUGS EDUCATION EXPERIENCES OF YOUNG PEOPLE

Of particular concern is the perceived ease of accessibility to alcohol and tobacco by under-age drinkers and smokers, from a number of commercial outlets and their own homes. This is something that can be addressed only by parents and schools working closely with local authority efforts to monitor and prevent illegal sales to minors. Parents' own use of legal drugs also appears to be a factor in their children's subsequent behaviour around legal substances (HEA 1992). This knowledge needs sensitive handling by schools in seeking partnerships with parents to address drugs issues, but should be available in the public domain. Most parents would not want to adversely affect school efforts towards demand reduction through ignorance of their own contribution in addressing the problems. Education programmes designed to support parents in modelling appropriate behaviour around drugs, and involving them as joint educators with schools, could send coherent messages to young people.

The knowledge that regular use of alcohol and tobacco and dependent tobacco use also appear to be correlated with use of illegal drugs also provides pointers for school drugs education provision – specifically, the need for educational measures to focus on alcohol and tobacco in the primary school, preferably before first experimentation. Drugs education in secondary schools also needs to take account of the findings of multi-drug use, and the implications of this behaviour for short- and long-term health. The social context of alcohol and tobacco use also needs to be addressed within drugs education. From the survey it is clear that this is largely a social activity, taking place at social occasions such as parties, and with friends.

The first-hand findings also serve to illuminate national and local surveys which appear to indicate that illegal drugs use is common amongst secondary school pupils. By looking at the reported level of illegal drug use it has been possible to get a clearer picture of this. Thus, it was ascertained that only 17 per cent of young people in the sample had at some point tried an illicit drug. This does not suggest that illegal drugs use is 'normal' amongst secondary school pupils, and indicates that some research may have lumped all levels of illegal drug use together, possibly giving a false picture of normalization of drugs use (Paraskeva 1995).

However, more respondents have tried cannabis then report ever having tried a drug, suggesting that for a small minority cannabis is not considered to be a drug, far less a dangerous one. Furthermore, 39 per cent considered it easy to get hold of cannabis, and 35 per cent of the older age group agreed with its legalization. Despite this only 17 per cent think 'drugs are OK if you are careful', and only 9 per cent think 'taking drugs is just a bit of fun'. This suggests that illegal drugs are a reality in young people's lives, but in general they do not treat them casually. Cannabis is overwhelmingly the illegal drug of use, and, as it is generally smoked, may help to explain the strong link between dependent tobacco smoking and cannabis use. In terms of 'what works' at least in terms of meeting young people's needs, interventions need to take account of these findings which are located in young people's perceptions and experience of drugs and drugs education.

THE WAY FORWARD AND SOME 'FIRST PRINCIPLES' TO INFORM DRUGS EDUCATION

The first-hand findings support sources in the literature which show that drugs education in schools is generally a piecemeal affair. So far there is little evidence of sustained, coherent programmes based on 'best practice' identified from the literature and outlined in SCAA/DfE (1995) policy documents. (See also Chapter 7.) However, the young people surveyed are generally positive about drugs education, although they wish for it to be more closely matched to their needs and experience. This is particularly true for those with first-hand experience of drugs, who were least likely to have found provision useful so far.

The gender and ethnic effects indicate that focused education efforts could usefully take account of the findings that girls are more likely to drink alcohol and smoke tobacco more frequently than boys. Similarly, white children are more likely then non-white to engage in legal and illegal drug use; this remains true for each ethnic group surveyed. These findings support other research which has refuted the stereotypical images of black drug use (Ramsey and Percey 1996).

The need for drugs educators to acknowledge and incorporate the experience, perceptions and motivations of young people relating to drugs (Hirst and McCamley-Finney 1994), is further supported by the research. The knowledge that young people overwhelmingly give their reasons for drug taking as 'enjoyment', 'to help relax' and 'to feel good' provides an important starting point for educational inputs. Equally, the understanding that drug use almost always takes place in a social context (raves, parties, pubs, clubs, bars, parks) allows educators to plan education provision that incorporates interpersonal skills training designed to make drug refusal a realistic choice. This is particularly important given the related findings that 'friends' and 'acquaintances' are the most likely source of drugs.

The findings also indicate to educators that the priorities for young people are drug appearances and effects, street names for drugs, and sources of help for drugs problems. The latter indicates the need for drugs counselling agencies to be involved at some level in school policies and programmes. This is further supported by the finding that, if help was needed with a drugs problem, the majority (56 per cent), would go to a best friend, followed by a parent 28 per cent, and a teacher 18 per cent. None of these is likely to have specialist drugs counselling expertise, although all need to know how to access specialist agencies. A very small minority report taking drugs because they cannot stop. Nevertheless, school policies and programmes should take account of this minority, though working with counselling agencies to provide access to specialists.

Inevitably these findings pose issues for policy makers in schools, and external policy makers responsible for the major contributions to school drugs education; the latter are mainly police officers. These contributions include the need to identify and prepare those individuals with the necessary knowledge and expertise to deliver drugs education within planned, co-ordinated provision, properly resourced and supported. In order to be effective in any terms, drugs education programmes must be located within a credible rationale: this means drawing on research evidence and reflections on professional practice. A multi-faceted approach to drugs education based on an extensive review of the literature on the evaluation of intervention programmes and informed by the above findings is presented below. This is intended not as the final arbiter of 'what works' in this field (future research may move this on) but as an example of the key knowledge to date that policy makers and practitioners should bring to their efforts, if gains are to be made in young people's knowledge and understanding of drugs issues, and their safety and responsibility around drugs.

FIRST PRINCIPLES FOR DRUGS EDUCATION

- Start drugs education early, using interactive as well as knowledge-based approaches.
- Use young people's knowledge, experience and perceptions of drugs and drugs issues, and their expressed needs in this area, as a starting point, and incorporate these into planning, content and teaching methods.
- Provide long-term, sustained education, linked with developing knowledge and experience, changing perceptions and attitudes, and understanding of social and psychological development.
- Target information and approaches towards specific needs and groups, considering for example, gender, ethnic, cultural, social factors.
- Select well-trained, confident and credible deliverers.
- Ensure the school ethos and management structure is supportive in terms of resourcing, time commitment and coherent and cohesive messages about health and drugs.

- Involve and educate parents to support school efforts.
- Establish aims, objectives and outcomes of drugs education programmes, in collaboration with parents and external agencies, and clarify the contribution of each.
- Harness multi-agency contributions as part of a planned, coherent approach, which includes a policy to address drugs incidents in schools.
- Ensure school efforts are part of wider community efforts to reduce the availability and acceptability of drugs.
- Establish monitoring and evaluation procedures to measure success or inform necessary changes.

CONCLUSIONS

There are two themes running through each of the information collection methods employed in the study – that the current level and form of provision is not sufficient or appropriate but that there is good will and enthusiasm on the part of many of those involved in the provision of drugs education in schools to improve this. It is encouraging that many of those involved in drugs education are working towards developing more appropriate methods. An essentially optimistic message is justified by evidence of good practice in some schools, the desire for drugs education amongst young people and the development of some community-based approaches in which those within and without the school are working collaboratively to improve the provision available to young people.

However, it is critical that this development of community-wide drugs education is managed in a manner that is consistent with the educational objectives of parents, teachers and outside agencies as well as young people. For this reason it is also necessary that the process is an open and partici-pative one in which the views of each group are regularly sought and that each is involved in the decision making procedure. With the young people, it is crucial that their levels of awareness and activities with regard to illicit substance use (as well as alcohol and tobacco) are regularly assessed so that the interventions can be pitched at a suitable level. It is through this form of needs assessment, rather than prescriptive policy making, that informed decisions can be reached about the appropriate age for initiating interventions and deciding on the philosophy and content of these sessions. Similarly, a regular procedure for consultation and assessment would most readily permit evaluation of the effectiveness of interventions as a standard component of drugs education, rather than as an infrequent luxury. A move towards drugs education based on evaluations of efforts so far, clear aims, objectives and intended outcomes, tested through systematic monitoring and evaluation, would enable drugs educators to focus efforts more productively. Such programmes are most likely to 'work' at least in the terms specified.

REFERENCES

Blackman, S. (1996) *Drugs Education and the National Curriculum: An Evaluation of 'Drug Studies: A Resource for the National Curriculum'.* Drugs Prevention Initiative, Paper 11. London: HMSO.

Canavan, D. (1995) Unpublished paper presented in part fulfilment for the

Certificate in Substance Misuse: Prevention and Education, Roehampton Institute London.

Coggans, N.D., Shewan, D., Henderson, M., Davies, J.B. and O'Hagen, F.J. (1991) *National Evaluation of Drug Education in Scotland: Final Report.* Edinburgh: Scottish Education Department.

Coggans, N. and Watson, J. (1995), Drug education: approaches, effectiveness and delivery. *Drugs, Education, Prevention and Policy.* **2**, 211–24.

Department for Education (1995) *Drug Prevention and Schools.* Circular 4/95. London: DfE.

Department for Education and the School Curriculum and Assessment Authority (1995) *Drug Education: Curriculum Guidance for Schools* London: SCAA/DfE.

Dobson, B. (1995) *A Consultative Project on the Effective Implementation of Drug Education in 5 European Countries.* Salford. TACADE.

Dowds, L. and Redfern, J. (1994) *Drug Education amongst Teenagers: A 1992 British Crime Survey Analysis,* Research Planning Unit, Paper 86. London: HMSO.

Health Advisory Service (1996) *Children and Young People: An NHS Health Advisory Service Thematic Review.* London: HMSO.

Health Education Authority (1992) *Tomorrow's Young Adults: 9–15 Year Olds Look at Alcohol, Drugs, Exercise and Smoking.* London: MORI.

Hirst, J. and McCamley-Finney, F. (1994) *The Place and Meaning of Drugs in the Lives of Young People.* Health Research Institute Report No. 7, Sheffield: Hallam University.

Institute for the Study of Drug Dependence (1994) *Drug Misuse in Britain in 1994.* London. ISDD.

Kent County Constabulary (1995) *Misuse of Drugs: A Survey of 11–17 Year Olds in Kent, December 1994–January 1995.* Maidstone: Kent County Council Education Department.

Kinder, B.N., Pape, N.E. and Walfish, S. (1980) Drug and alcohol education programmes: a review of outcome studies. *International Journal of Addiction,* **15**, 1035–54.

Noble, C. (1996) Beyond the health promoting school. *Health Education.* **1**, 16–19.

O'Connor, L. (1991) Health education: feeling the squeeze. *Education and Health,* **9**(2), 28–31.

O'Connor, D. (1992). Developing a partnership approach for drugs education. In Evans, R. and O'Connor, L. (eds), *Drug Abuse and Misuse: Developing Educational Strategies in Partnership.* Roehampton Institute Occasional Papers 1. London: David Fulton.

O'Connor, L. (1995) Drug education in schools: getting it right. Paper presented to the London Drugs Policy Forum Conference, 24 March 1995, *Youth Culture – Drug Culture.* London: Drugs Policy Forum

O'Connor, L., Best, D., Best, R. and Rowley, J. (1997) *Young People, Drugs and Drugs Education: Missed Opportunities.* Report of a collaborative research project into three London Boroughs: Merton, Sutton and Wandsworth. London: Roehampton Institute.

Office for Standards in Education (1997) *Drug Education in Schools.* London: HMSO.

Paraskeva, J. (1995) Drugs from a young person's perspective. Paper presented to the London Drug Policy Forum Conference, 24 March 1995, *Youth Culture – Drug Culture*. London: Drugs Policy Forum.

Ramsey, M. and Percey, A. (1996) *Drug Misuse Declared: Results of the 1994 British Crime Survey*. Research Findings No. 36. London: HMSO.

Shiner, M. and Newburn, T. (1996) *Young People, Drugs and Peer Education: An Evaluation of the Youth Awareness Programme (YAP)*. Home Office Drug Prevention Initiative, Paper No. 13. London: HMSO.

Sidebottom, D. (1995) School health education: do too many cooks spoil the broth? *Health Education*, **6**, 17– 23.

Stead, M., Hastings, G. and Tudor-Smith, C. (1996) Preventing adolescent smoking: a review of options. *Health Education Journal*, **55**, 31–54.

Swadi, H. (1988) Substance use among 3,333 London adolescents. *British Journal of Addiction*, **85**, 935–42.

Wetton, N. (1992) Primary school children and the world of drugs. In White Paper (1995), *Tackling Drugs Together: A Strategy for England 1995–1998*. CMD 2846. London: HMSO.

White Paper (1995) *Tackling Drugs Together: A Practical Digest for Drug Action Teams*. London: CDCU, HMSO.

White Paper (1995) *Tackling Drugs Together. A Strategy for England 1995–1998*. CMD 2846. London: HMSO.

Williams, T., Wetton, N.M. and Moon, A. (1989), *A Picture of Health*. London: HEA.

Wragg, J. (1992) National Campaign Against Drug Abuse. In *An Evaluation of a Model of Drug Education*. Monograph Series No. 22. Canberra: Australian Government Publishing Service.

CHAPTER 7

Drugs policies in schools: moving from statements of intent to effective action

Louise O'Connor, Jenny Rowley, Paul Wotton and Vivienne Evans

INTRODUCTION

Education is clearly identified as a central component of the drugs strategy outlined in the 1995 government White Paper, *Tackling Drugs Together*. Thus one of the key objectives of the strategy is to: 'reduce the acceptability and availability of drugs to young people'. The means whereby schools are to assist in this major objective are set out in the DfE Circular 4/95, *Drug Prevention and Schools*, which was made available to all maintained and independent schools in 1995. A recently published Ofsted (Office For Standards in Education) inspection report (1997) appears to demonstrate the success of Circular 4/95 in influencing the majority of maintained schools to establish drugs policies. The report found that over 40 per cent of primary and 70 per cent of secondary schools had recently either reviewed or written new policies on drugs education. Furthermore, schools had notably increased the number of policies for drug-related incidents throughout 1996, with such policies existing in 74 per cent of secondary schools and 30 per cent of primary schools. All of this looks positive for the development and implementation of effective drugs policies in schools.

However, a closer look at the Ofsted report, the wider literature and some first-hand research carried out by Roehampton Institute London in collaboration with Merton, Sutton and Wandsworth Health Authority illustrates the difficulties in assessing whether policies as *statements of intent* are being translated into *effective action*.

Action for Governors' Information and Training (1995) has summarized the choices for school policies as follows:

A policy can be a piece of paper written without commitment and kept on a shelf with no-one remembering which shelf. It can also be a vital management tool, thoughtfully written, used daily, regularly reviewed and readily available to members of the school community, including parents.

This chapter will examine critically the supportive and inhibiting factors for achieving the second definition of a policy which addresses drug: and drug-related incidents. This necessitates an examination of ke: policy formulation and implementation, including the rationale ur policies, the management of change, inter-agency collaboration, evaluation and the wider social policy context both national and local.

THE RATIONALE – WHAT ARE WE TRYING TO ACHIEVE?

Circular 4/95 accepts that schools cannot 'solve' the problems of drug misuse and the young, but nevertheless sees drug misuse as an educational issue which can and should be addressed by schools. Schools are seen as pivotal in 'tackling' rising trends in drugs misuse amongst the young, and both primary and secondary schools in urban and rural areas are given notice that there are no 'no-go areas for illegal drugs'. The clear intention behind the Circular is to galvanize schools into concerted action by stating that drugs are an issue for all schools, not just those in deprived inner cities. Thus, 'The aim is to encourage better planned and targeted practice in this important area and to counter the stigma which has too often attached to schools who have made a stand against drugs.'

However, the ultimate aim of school policies must be seen in the broader context of the White Paper. Drugs *prevention* is defined here as incorporating both 'primary prevention' (stopping drugs experimentation in the first place) and 'secondary prevention' (treatment and rehabilitation to help those who are misusing drugs to stop). The concept of *harm reduction* (assisting those who are resistant to ending drug-using behaviour to adopt safer practices) as a legitimate aim of school drugs policies is nowhere clearly addressed. This is a potential difficulty for schools in reconciling the aims and values of school policies modelled on advice contained in the Circular and the needs of a minority of young people who are persistent drug users. The companion document to the Circular, *Drug Education: Curriculum Guidance for Schools*, is similarly silent on this.

However, there is evidence of a fairly pragmatic approach to individual school policies contained in the latter document, which, whilst advising schools that 'a healthy lifestyle' is the preferred context for drugs education, rather than programmes which rely on 'slogans or vivid and frightening images' does not provide a prescriptive approach. Instead schools should 'consider' including the following in their education programmes:

- information about drugs and health that gives accurate and up-to-date coverage of the effects of drugs and the risks and legal aspects of drug taking;
- opportunities for pupils to develop their abilities to communicate, assert themselves and take responsible decisions, identify risks and help others, thereby enhancing their competence and self-esteem.

The above appear to reflect the commonsense view of what it is possible for schools to achieve. Such school efforts may not result in demonstrable long-term behavioural and attitudinal changes relating to drug use and misuse, but they may be able to demonstrate increased knowledge and awareness of drugs and drugs issues, and the acquisition of key skills required by young people to exercise real choices on health and drugs decisions. In recognition of this, Ofsted (1997) acknowledges that evaluation of the long-term behaviour changes of individuals is beyond the remit of individual schools or LEAs (Local Education Authorities).

In summary, there is some lack of clarity in terms of the underpinning rationale for school drugs policies. Whilst clear themes emerge, including the intention to reduce the acceptability and availability of drugs, the need for co-ordinated action, partnership issues and the desirability of well-planned, coherent drugs education, there are some mixed messages relating to the relative contribution of schools to the overall national drugs strategy, and the status and credibility of policies themselves. For example, the policies hold a somewhat nebulous position within the statutory school curriculum framework. Drugs education may be an aspect of the Science National Curriculum (albeit a minor one), and school policies are subject to monitoring by Ofsted. However, there is no statutory framework for Personal, Social and Health Education within which drugs education should arguably be addressed, and institutions providing initial teacher education are not required to produce teacher 'experts' to lead this area. School action therefore generally depends on individual organizational and personal commitment, leading to generally patchy provision with somewhat isolated examples of good practice (Ofsted 1997; O'Connor 1995).

The underlying weaknesses in the thinking that underpins school drugs policies, coupled with planning and development issues, necessitates a consideration of the wider literature relating to inter-agency collaboration, evaluation of drugs education interventions and management of change factors, when assessing the likelihood of sound drugs policies emerging in the majority of schools.

PARTNERSHIPS: SCHOOLS, PARENTS AND MULTI-AGENCY COLLABORATION

In order to assist schools to develop sound policies, Circular 4/95 includes detailed guidance on the principles and practice of drugs education, the use of outside speakers, the involvement of parents and school governors, policy co-ordination at school and local level, teacher training issues and the role of Ofsted in monitoring provision. Examples of policies and education content are included as appendices, together with information on drugs and the law and excerpts from other documentation relating to young people's drug use. Whilst much of the advice given is not contentious, the management of drug-related incidents is addressed in some detail, and this is an area likely to bring schools into conflict with parents if managed insensitively, as a case example reported in the *TES* demonstrated (see *TES* 1995).

Dealing with drugs incidents
The Circular attempts to achieve a considered and balanced response to drugs incidents by dealing with examples of misuse within the context of health and safety, pastoral care and school discipline policies. There is also encouragement to develop 'a repertoire of responses, incorporating both sanctions and counselling' to reflect the range of individual situations which schools may be

called upon to deal with. The involvement of external agencies is recommended, as a medium for sharing information and receiving advice and as a source of support for 'at risk' pupils. (See also Metropolitan Police 1996.) Overall, the guidance leaves much to the discretion of head teachers and governors, whilst discouraging a 'knee-jerk' reaction which over-relies on exclusions. However, the advice pertaining to teacher advice to pupils and confidentiality issues is potentially problematic: 'Where a pupil discloses to a teacher that he or she is taking drugs the teacher should make clear to the pupil that he or she can offer no guarantee of confidentiality given the seriousness of drug misuse.' That pupils perceive teachers as being in a difficult position as regards confidentiality and drugs is demonstrated by their reluctance to seek help from teachers if they have problems with drugs (O'Connor *et al.* 1997). Clarification is needed from the DfEE on teachers' legal position relating to advice in particular circumstances, so that this can be reflected in school policies. Failure to clarify the situation leaves pupils, parents, teachers and governors in a potentially untenable position.

Involving key partners

The themes of consultation and co-ordination are clearly identified throughout the advice given. Partnerships with parents and key agencies such as health, social services and the police are seen as crucial to the success of policies. For example, 'Schools will need the support and encouragement of parents in their efforts on drug prevention'. Schools are encouraged to hold information evenings where parents can learn about the school's approach to drugs and drugs education. Furthermore, school efforts are seen as part of wider community initiatives to educate parents about drugs issues. School governors are also identified as having a 'key role' in their school's policy development, and their training needs accordingly identified. External speakers are acknowledged as having a useful role to play in school drugs education, but not as teacher substitutes. To this end the Circular clearly identifies schools and teachers as leading this curriculum area, supported by visiting 'experts':

> Where outside speakers are involved, their contribution must have been properly planned as part of an overall programme. Their contribution should complement other teaching, the tone and substance should match the age and maturity of the pupils involved, and teachers should always be involved so they are able to deal with any follow-up questions or concerns.

But potentially helpful as this plethora of advice may be, recent research conducted at the Roehampton Institute of London into the needs and concerns of parents in relation to their children's potential and actual drug use uncovered widespread ignorance of local school policies and approaches adopted within drugs education (see Chapter 3). There was little evidence of systematic school efforts to consult with parents on the aims and content of policies, or to inform them of the key components of the finished products. In addition, little evidence has emerged to indicate that visitors to the classroom are 'complementing' well-planned, co-ordinated programmes as envisaged in Circular 4/95 (Canavan 1995; Green 1995). In contrast, 'one-off' inputs appear to be the norm.

The latter is particularly significant when the Circular's advice to schools on dealing with drug-related incidents recommends the involvement of police and other support agencies. A coherent policy should ensure that messages within educational contexts complement planned responses to incidents, which are themselves informed by pastoral and school discipline policies (Chapman 1992). Positive relationships between school, parents and community agencies require a thoughtful, structured approach which clearly identifies joint aims, values and desired outcomes (TACADE/LDPF 1996).

Agreeing approaches

The problem of agreeing joint aims, values and intended outcomes for overall policies is complicated by the current variety of approaches to drugs education in British schools. Owing to the lack of trained teachers in health and drugs education, there is often no in-house 'expert' to guide and lead whole innovations in this area. Thus some schools have welcomed the input of external agencies and individuals into drugs education provision without assessing the educational value of the programmes and/or approaches they represent. This is a particular problem with high-profile American- and/or Australian-inspired programmes which have not been shown to significantly increase drugs knowledge, reduce drug experimentation, or change attitudes (Coggans and Watson 1995). The danger with these is that schools may be persuaded to collaborate in programmes that are educationally unsound to the detriment of long-term sustained drugs education which is modelled on advice in the Circular and related SCAA/DfEE documentation. This is a problem which can only be addressed if the contributing agencies closely match their inputs to the official advice given to schools. (See for example, ACPO 1996.)

The Circular extends the partnership approach to include LEA advice on drugs policies (where these exist) and strategic decisions of Drug Action Teams (DATs). These were set up under the auspices of the White Paper, and comprising senior policy makers from all the key agencies, including education, health, social services and police, and evidence is now emerging of co-ordinated action on school policies precipitated by DAT strategies (see, for example, Wandsworth Drug Action Team 1996). The influence of DATs on this area is as yet untested on a large scale, but, if monitoring of policies can be established at local level, there is potential for overseeing policy statements translated into practice, introducing a measure of local accountability into schools.

The establishment of DATs and the advisory Drugs Reference Groups provide a framework within which partnerships can operate. Nevertheless, it is important to recognize that differing values and agendas of organizations can inhibit effective collaboration. Bloxham (1996) has identified agreement about aims, identification of common values, a common vision, effective personal and professional relationships, effective facilitation of joint action and shared or relevant training as positives for successful partnerships. The negatives include ignorance of other professions, protective attitude towards professional image and status, defence of personal autonomy, narrow vision and lack of co-ordination. However, it may not be necessary for organizations with different objectives – education and crime control for example – to share all the same values. The Advisory Council on the Misuse of Drugs provides a realistic and workable model for agencies with different rationales in the 1994 publication, *Police, Drug Users and the Community*:

At the operational level, there is a need for agencies to develop local alliances to plan and implement specific programmes of action. We use the word alliance deliberately, with its connotation of a temporary association where the common object and the mutual benefit is stated and defines what is affected by the agreement. It allows for considerable differences between allies in those parts of their work which have no relevance to the common object.

Some examples from a 1995/6 collaborative research project between Roehampton Institute London and Merton, Sutton and Wandsworth Health Authority provide further illustrations of the problems in developing effective partnerships between schools and external agencies to develop coherent action.

CASE STUDY: A COLLABORATIVE RESEARCH PROJECT IN THREE LONDON BOROUGHS

As part of a research project into young people's knowledge, perceptions and experiences of drugs and drugs education in three London boroughs, undertaken by Roehampton Institute London, a sample of providers of drugs education were questioned about the nature of the drugs education they offered, and whether this was part of a multi-agency approach located within a whole-school drugs policy. In all a dozen interviews were held with key individuals, including police schools' liaison officers, primary and secondary school teacher co-ordinators of PSHE (Personal, Social and Health Education) and health promotion officers. In addition sixteen teachers (predominantly primary with some secondary) completed a questionnaire designed to elicit their views on the implementation of drugs policies and education in their schools. Finally a dissemination exercise of the initial research findings provided an opportunity for focus groups of teachers, governors and multi-agency representatives to give feedback to researchers on what they considered necessary for moving this area forward.

Multi-agency perspectives
The research uncovered a high degree of agreement amongst teachers, police officers and health professionals contributing to school drugs education on the need for changes. For example, the need for more focused programmes, matching the needs of young people, was identified as a main area for improvement. There was also a high degree of consensus on preferred teaching approaches based on factual information; scare tactics were favoured by none.

Almost without exception, respondents believed that a combination of teachers and external speakers to be the best way of delivering drugs education, and that this made possible the exploration of broad perspectives on drugs. However, time and resource constraints allowed external visitors into classes of children approximately once a year. Multi-agency networks were generally considered to be 'a good thing' and suggested as 'the way forward' in drugs education. Nevertheless, multi-agency work often appeared poorly co-ordinated, with lessons conducted as 'one-offs' not as part of a co-operative effort within a planned school drugs education programme. Finally a number of respondents reported that agencies had different agendas, which could work against co-ordinated action. Evaluation of either school or multi-agency efforts also appeared to be non-existent, reflecting a situation identified in the Ofsted (1997) report.

Teacher responses

Only one teacher (primary) claimed to have a completed drugs policy, which addressed both education and drug-related incidents. All the others were either at the planning stage or in draft form, with some pilot implementation. However, one primary teacher reported that her school had held parents' meetings and governor training, and the writing of the policy was in process. Other schools (primary and secondary) referred to consultation with teachers, parents and governors as part of the development of a whole school policy. Primary teachers in particular seemed aware of the importance of involving the whole school in policy development. An additional significant finding indicated that teachers in schools using PSHE as a main or equal-status subject for drugs education accorded a higher status to drugs education than those schools using alternative curriculum subjects. Overall some encouraging signs were identified, with evidence that schools recognized the importance of consultation to successful policy implementation.

Teacher expertise

Despite, the encouraging signs of emerging drugs policies, several teachers (primary and secondary) expressed reservations about their capability to deliver drugs education. For example, eight of the primary school teachers had had no training for drugs education at all. Where training had occurred, this had tended to be on a piecemeal, random basis, consisting of a few days here and there. Many of the primary teachers were unsure of the school's agreed approach to drugs education, and several suggested that this did not exist. However, the majority of primary teachers considered that primary schools should address this area. Despite feeling insufficiently trained for the task, they considered that primary teachers to be suitable providers of drugs education. A similar picture emerged from the secondary teachers, The training provided, so far, appeared to have been inconsistent and limited. The teachers expressed mixed feelings about the quality of drugs education on offer in their schools. They accepted that drugs education was a necessary part of secondary school education, but the general belief was that more training, resources and support were necessary to improve provision.

The dissemination exercise

The dissemination of the initial research findings gave an opportunity for teachers, governors and external agencies to illuminate further the problems and issues in taking forward policies as statements of intent into everyday practice. The key individuals contributing to focus groups identified a number of factors likely to prove critical to the adoption of sound policies. These included increased community involvement (with an emphasis on the role of parents), and greater prioritization of drugs issues in school curriculums matched by increased resources. In the primary groups emphasis was placed on starting drugs education at an early age. The favoured approach was identified as long-term, progressive and consistent, enhancing relationships between teachers and children.

Participants stated that increased support for teachers was an essential component of any measure that required their commitment to the process. It was also felt that improved communication between external contributors, teachers, governors and parents would augment the consistency of key messages and support the development of coherent and workable drugs policies. Many teacher contributors emphasized a need for more information about training opportunities and available resources.

Similar views were expressed by governors, who also believed that increased co-operation and communication with parents and teachers would prove beneficial. They also proved supportive of the need for external visitors to be involved within a coherent and clearly defined policy outline.

Overall a high level of awareness was demonstrated by the individuals present, of the need for focused action at all levels if the desired result is to be effective in school policies. The following quotations from the final evaluation exercise illustrate perceptions of what needs to be done in terms of information, support and the wider policy context:

Now we know what we could, should be doing, we need to know what LEA and National Government will do in practical ways to support all schools. 90 per school in GEST is not enough! There must be enough money/resources for whole school approach and outside. Also help with policy documents. Information – Who? Where? etc. Information from outside agencies.

Drugs education is only a part of the whole area of PSHE which is not recognized as part of the National Curriculum. It is therefore very important to recognize PSHE as a curriculum area so that teachers can do justice to it, as it underpins life skills. You can't teach drugs education in isolation.

PSHE co-ordinators meeting with multi-agencies to discuss effective drugs programmes that work! A discussion of best practice between school PSHE co-ordinators.

PSHE co-ordinators would like time out of class possibly with others to create schemes of work which are progressive and cover all aspects of drugs education linked to resources.

MANAGEMENT OF CHANGE

The above findings from first-hand research illustrate the real issues in translating policy as intent into effective action within educational organizations. For example several writers in the field, including Bolam (1975) and Fullan (1982), have identified some key questions for assessing the likelihood of successful policy implementation:

- Does a clear understanding of the change process exist?
- Are the necessary skills and knowledge available to carry through the change?

- Are resources available to support the change, for example training and teaching materials, time for planning and reviewing?
- How committed are the implementers of the change process to the change itself?
- Is there clear direction from those who have initiated the change?

The first-hand research presented here, and the Ofsted report (1997), clearly indicate that the above criteria are lacking in certain significant areas of policy planning. Whilst elements of good practice have been identified, especially where commitment to PSHE or drugs education is apparent, schools do not generally provide the managerial conditions in which effective drugs policies can flourish. This appears to be a particular problem for the non-statutory health-related curriculum (Dobson 1995; HEA/NFER 1993; O'Connor 1991). Schools are subject to financial constraints on resources, and in the light of this inevitably prioritize those curriculum areas which they are statutorily bound to deliver. Whilst the SCAA and DfE guidance documents make it clear that the minimum requirements of the Science National Curriculum provide inadequate coverage of drugs issues, it is perhaps inevitable that some schools will limit their input to this.

In summary a review of the literature, coupled with first-hand research and lessons from the management of change, suggests that, in order for the supportive conditions to exist for effective school drugs policies to become part of everyday school practice, action at every level is needed – specifically, at national (government) level, DATs with local authorities, and senior management (including governing bodies) at school level.

National government
Health education, including Personal, Social and Health Education (PSHE), needs to become part of the National Curriculum, externally examined through GCSE examination. This would ensure the provision of appropriate qualifications within initial teacher education, resulting in the emergence of health education curriculum experts to lead and co-ordinate this area. Long-term resource allocation in recognition of the statutory position would enable schools to plan accordingly, providing curriculum co-ordinators, in-service training and resource materials. Accrediting training based on national standards also needs to be provided for practising teachers and external drugs educators. Quality control is clearly needed, to establish some consistency of provision of drugs education in schools informed by identified best practice. (See Chapter 9.)

Local authorities
The DATs have a crucial role to play in the strategic planning for this area. They can put school policies centre stage within DAT strategies, working in partnership with all key agencies on jointly agreed aims and intended outcomes. There are already examples of the DATs' influence on a range of drug-related activities: mobilizing agencies and communities to focus on the contribution schools can make to drugs issues could make a significant impact (CDCU 1996). Commissioning information gathering to establish baselines, raising awareness of parents, teachers, agencies and communities of the need

for action, establishing targets for policies with LEAs and monitoring provision, implementation and impact of policies could all assist in meeting their major objectives of reducing the availability and acceptability of drugs.

Schools

At school level there are a number of ways in which senior managers and governing bodies, supported by national and local initiatives, could ensure that drugs policies are incorporated into the working life of the school. For example they could:

- demonstrate commitment by prioritizing drugs policies within school development plans;
- ensure capability to plan, implement, co-ordinate and evaluate provision through the allocation of resources, particularly training and time;
- provide a supportive school climate, in which the school ethos favours positive health messages;
- use all channels of communication to involve parents, the whole school community and beyond, including the local media, to support school efforts.

CONCLUSION

This chapter has focused on the reality of changing school drugs policies from well-intentioned statements of intent into practical, effective working documents which inform school practice on a day-to-day basis. The literature and first-hand research have indicated that promising beginnings have been made, but, without concerted efforts on behalf of government, DATs and local authorities, and schools themselves, the quantity of policies may not reflect their quality. Circular 4/95, *Drugs Prevention and Schools*, has undoubtedly moved the issue forward, but there is still some way to go. In its own words:

> This Circular reflects recognised good practice in schools and offers guidance on the principles which should inform the development of school drug education programmes and assist schools in dealing effectively and consistently with drug related incidents. Each school will want to consider its own response to drug prevention in the light of these common principles.

As a guidance document the Circular provides a helpful framework to schools formulating drugs policies. But if the intention is to achieve a management tool central to the working of the school, then stronger measures are needed. Located within a statutory obligation, these measures must be supported by adequate resources to support schools in the development of commitment and capability to address drugs issues.

REFERENCES

Action for Governors' Information and Training (1995) *How to Write School Policies*. School Governors' Do-it-better Guide. Coventry: AGIT.

Advisory Council on the Misuse of Drugs (1993) *Drug Education in Schools: The Need for New Impetus*. London: HMSO.

Advisory Council on the Misuse of Drugs (1994) *Drug Misuse and the Criminal Justice System: Policy, Drug Users and the Community.* London: HMSO.

Association of Chief Police Officers (1996) *The ACPO National Drugs Strategy.* Wakefield, West Yorkshire: ACPO Crime Drugs Sub-Committee.

Bloxham, S. (1996) A case study of inter-agency collaboration in the education and promotion of young people's sexual health. *Health Education Journal,* **55**, 389–403.

Bolam, S. (1975) The management of educational change: towards a conceptual framework. In Houghton, V., McHugh, R. and Morgan, C. (1975) *The Management of Organisations and Individuals.* London: Open University Press.

Canavan, D. (1995), Unpublished paper presented in part fulfilment for the Certificate in Substance Misuse: Prevention and Education, Roehampton Institute London.

Central Drugs Co-ordination Unit (1996), *One Year on.* London: HMSO.

Chapman, C. (1992), *Drugs Issues for Schools* (revised 1995). London: ISDD.

Coggans, N. and Watson, J. (1995) Drug education: approaches, effectiveness and delivery. *Drugs, Education, Prevention and Policy,* **2**, 211– 24.

Department for Education (1995) *Drug Prevention and Schools.* Circular 4/95. London: DfE.

Department for Education and the School Curriculum and Assessment Authority (1995) *Drug Education: Curriculum Guidance for Schools.* London: SCAA/DfE.

Dobson, B. (1995), *A Consultative Project on the Effective Implementation of Drug Education in 5 European Countries.* Salford: TACADE.

Fullan, M. (1982) Research into educational innovation. In Gray, H.L. (ed.), *The Management of Educational Institutions.* London: Falmer Press.

Green, A. (1995) *The Role of the Police in Drug Education in Schools.* Unpublished MA Thesis, University of Exeter.

Health Education Authority/National Foundation for Educational Research (1993) *A Survey of Health Education Policies in Schools.* London: HEA.

Metropolitan Police (1996) *Guidelines to Police Involvement in Drug Related Incidents in Schools.* London: Community Safety and Partnership Policy Unit (CO2O), New Scotland Yard.

O'Connor, L. (1991), Health education: feeling the squeeze. *Education and Health,* **9**(2), 28–31.

O'Connor, L. (1995), Drug education in schools: getting it right. Paper presented to the London Drugs Policy Forum Conference, 24 March 1995, *Youth Culture – Drug Culture.* London: Drugs Policy Forum.

O'Connor, L., Best, D.W., Best, R.M. and Rowley, J. (1997) *Young People, Drugs and Drugs Education: Missed Opportunities.* Report of a collaborative research project into three London Boroughs. London: Roehampton Institute London, Merton, Sutton and Wandsworth Health Authority.

Office For Standards in Education (1997) *Drug Education in Schools.* London: HMSO.

TACADE and London Drug Policy Forum (1996) *Making the Most of Visitors: Using Outside Agencies in School Drug Education.* Salford: TACADE/LGDF.

TES (1995) Talkback, Who's committed the crime here? A bewildered mother lists the injustices she feels her son suffered when he was expelled from school. *Times Educational Supplement*, TES 2, 19 May.

Wandsworth Drug Action Team (1996) *Tackling Drugs Together: A Strategy for Addressing Drug and Alcohol Misuse*. Consultation Document. London: Borough of Wandsworth.

Wandsworth Education Department (1996) *Drugs Issues and the Needs of Young People: Using local Research to Inform Drugs Education*. Conference Evaluation, 6 December. Wandsworth: Professional Development Centre.

CHAPTER 8

Getting it right: the case for risk education[1]

Jenny McWhirter, Noreen Wetton and Filiz Mortimer

THE CONTEXT OF DRUGS EDUCATION

The problem of effective drugs education has perplexed educators, both researchers and practitioners, for some time. Is drugs education effective if young people understand the difference between medicines and illegal drugs? Is drugs education effective if young people make informed choices, even if that choice is to use illegal or addictive substances? We still don't have all the answers. This chapter will address one aspect of drugs education which may contribute to the development of new strategies for working with young people in schools and in the wider community.

Health educators argue that to be effective drugs education should not be an isolated activity, and that it should take place in the context of a broader healthy lifestyles approach (Wetton 1992). The reasons for this are many, but relate principally to the epidemiological evidence of clustering of health risks. Evidence for this was recently reviewed by Aggleton (1995) and is supported by the findings of O'Connor, Best and Best (Chapter 6 above) that dependent smokers are more likely to use illicit drugs than non-smokers and that regular use of alcohol is associated with illicit drug use.

There are further associations between these activities and other risk behaviours such as the early onset of sexual behaviour. This suggests that while the content of a drugs education programme will have its own unique features, some aspects will overlap with other issues in health and safety education. One solution to this problem has been for curriculum developers to offer skills-based programmes (Hopson and Scally 1981).

There is strong evidence that knowledge change is a necessary, but not sufficient, basis for behaviour change (Baric 1996). Aggleton (1995), however, stresses the importance of programmes which are not purely skills-based but which also provide information about specific health issues. The difficulty health educators face is the co-ordination of skills and content within a programme in which the transferability and interplay of both knowledge and skills are explicit and recognized by children and young people.

USING 'DRAW AND WRITE' TO EXPLORE PERCEPTIONS OF RISK

We have been researching the extent to which this transference occurs by examining how people perceive and explain risk. Risk is a fundamental concept underpinning health education. We wanted to know how children and adults perceive and explain risk and to plot their changing perceptions of risky behaviour of all kinds.

Drugs education, whether it is delivered by teachers, police officers, school nurses or other professionals, focuses on providing young people with accurate information and the skills to make empowered, informed choices through classroom-based activity. The success of this is tested in real life at a club, or on a street corner, when a young person, perhaps already under the influence of alcohol and amongst a group of peers, must be able to:

- recognize a specific hazard;
- assess the risk;
- take decisions about managing the risk.

We began by finding out how children of primary school age perceive and explain risk, using a draw and write technique (Williams *et al.* 1989a, b; Wetton and McWhirter 1998).

Pupils were asked to draw someone their own age doing something risky. We asked the children to write what was happening in the picture, and to write what made the activity risky. Finally we asked the children to add to their picture by drawing themselves somewhere in the scene and to write what they would be saying or doing or thinking if they were there.

Children who could not write for themselves, or who were reluctant to do so, were encouraged to use adult scribes who were instructed to write down exactly what the pupils said about their picture. Quantitative data and qualitative data emerged which enabled us to discover both the categories of risk which primary school children described and a broad picture of the meaning of risk to this age group.

In early pilot studies (McWhirter and Wetton 1994) and a more recent unpublished study involving six hundred pupils in schools in Dorset and Hampshire we obtained similar findings.

THE FINDINGS: PRIMARY SCHOOL CHILDREN

Many of the youngest children had no understanding of the word 'risky', and, as permitted, in the research they wrote 'I don't know' on their papers. By the age of 8 the children appeared to have a distinctive understanding of the meaning of risk, which was characterized by immediate and severe outcomes such as jumping or falling from a high place or falling into shark-infested waters (see Figure 8.1a). Misbehaviour or naughtiness was also frequently depicted as risky (Figure 8.1b).

Children of primary school age associated 'risky' with 'dangerous', and often wrote: 'it is risky because it is dangerous'. The risk associated with misbehaviour was not a risk to physical health or safety but a risk to mental and emotional well-being. Children were risking the disapproval of their

Figure 8.1a A typical example of a child's response to the invitation to draw and write about someone their own age doing something risky

May 2ⁿᵈ

Girl
Age 10

P2
FG10 31.

CUPBOARD

Me raiding the biscut tin when mum told me not to touch it.

Q. What makes this riscy?
1. If mum catches me I will get smaked.

Figure 8.1b Misbehaviour was a feature of a primary-school-aged child's perception of risk

parents, teachers or other adult. This perception persisted to the top of the primary age range.

Aspects of risk which often form part of the primary school curriculum, such as road safety, home safety, water safety and stranger danger, were less frequently represented by the children in response to our invitations to draw and write. Health hazards such as smoking, alcohol and illegal drug use were absent from the first pilot studies in primary schools, although small numbers of children have included these in the more recent study.

The low association of health hazards and risk puzzled us since we knew from other studies (e.g. Williams *et al.* 1989b; McWhirter 1993; Oakley *et al.* 1995; Porcellato *et al.* 1996; Hughes *et al.* 1996; Chapter 6 of this volume) that children of primary school age have extensive knowledge of a variety of health hazards including drugs, puberty, cancer, smoking and the effects of sun on the skin. This suggests that teaching programmes do not help the children to make the links between specific health issues and the common skills needed to manage a wide range of risky situations.

A small study with teenage pupils suggested that the perception that risk is severe and short-term continues into adolescence, when risk-taking is typical behaviour (see Figure 8.2). This led us to question how mature adults perceive and explain risk.

ADULT PERCEPTIONS OF RISK

From a review of the literature it is clear that, amongst adults, lay and expert perceptions of risk differ. Experts, both safety specialists and professional risk takers, agree that the most severe outcome is not necessarily the most likely and therefore may be quantified as low-risk. In a recent article in the *Sunday Times* (12 January 1997) the explorer Sir Ranulph Fiennes claimed he was more likely to die at home, in bed, than in a desert or on an ice floe. It is little comfort to nervous air passengers, however, to be told that they are more likely to be killed in an accident on the road to the airport than in an air crash! Low-frequency events which have a severe outcome are classified by experts as low-risk, but media coverage given to air and road crashes may give the lay person a different perception.

Slovic *et al.* (1981) studied the bias which determines expert and lay perceptions of risk. Lay people were more likely to use hearsay or direct experience to inform their judgements about risk, while experts' opinions were more closely related to mortality statistics. This finding was underpinned by research into lay perceptions of risk in two cultures: Hungary and the USA (Englander *et al.* 1986). They found that people in the US sample were more concerned about high-tech risks such as radiation, nuclear power and chemical pollution, while the Hungarians were more concerned about the 'common, everyday, hazards of life' such as faulty electrical appliances and road accidents. The role of the press in these two societies at the time of the study may again have been influential, and risk perception can never be divorced from a consideration of the cultural, social and institutional contexts in which they are explored.

Slovic used a questionnaire approach to investigate perceptions of risk, so the possible risks were predetermined for the participants. Gibbons *et al.* (1995) have used prototype images to investigate perceptions of lifestyle risks amongst adolescents. Psychometric tests and structured questionnaires were used to determine how acceptable the prototype images were to the young people, and the results of these were compared with self-reports of the same risk behaviours. Adolescents who perceived the prototype in a positive way were more likely to report similar behaviour.

Both of these techniques, however, are closed-ended. The participants have no opportunity to say what risky behaviour means to them. The risky behav-

Figure 8.2 The idea that risk is short-term, with serious consequences, persists into adolescence

iour was defined by the experts and based, as Englander showed, on the mortality statistics.

We decided to extend the use of the open-ended 'draw and write' technique to tap into adult perceptions of risk. We included lay people and experts in our sample since we wanted to be able to describe a mature perception of risk, to compare with that of the children. This was the first time that the 'draw and write' technique had been used with adults in a formal study (Mortimer 1997).

CONTRASTING PERCEPTIONS OF RISK: ADULTS AND CHILDREN

There were clear distinctions between the adults' perceptions and the pupils' perceptions, summarized in Table 8.1.

Typical scenarios described by adults involved falls from a relatively low height, such as ladders, chairs or stairs, or in sports such as climbing where the risks were highly controlled (see Figure 8.3). Adults also depicted road accidents caused by drinking alcohol where other people were involved. Drug taking and unprotected sex featured strongly, especially amongst the younger female participants. Adults expressed positive views of risk, using expressions such as: 'that looks fun', or 'I'd like to have a go'. Such responses were rare amongst the primary school age range.

Perhaps the clearest contrast was in the category of misbehaviour or illegal behaviour (excluding drugs misuse, drinking and driving). While children associated risk with being caught or found out as the perpetrators of crime or misbehaviour, adults associated risk with being the victims of crime.

If this is how risk is perceived and explained, then what are the implications of these findings for health and, therefore, drugs education embedded in health education? We propose that there are four major issues to be addressed:

- Starting where people are
- Risk as a part of 'normal' behaviour
- Planning a spiral curriculum
- School as a health-promoting community

Starting where people are

If children of primary school age range are confused about risk and its meaning, we need to use concrete examples to help children construct a more mature understanding. It is not helpful to replace the word 'risk' with 'dangerous' when speaking to younger children, since this reinforces their misunderstanding that risk is synonymous with danger. It is not. Risk is associated with uncertainty, danger is associated with certainty, or at least very high probability – as depicted by the children when they draw people falling from high places. There are many opportunities in day-to-day classroom practice to introduce the words 'risk' or 'risky'. For example we might say to a class: 'It is dangerous to run about with those scissors, they will cut you.' Or 'It is risky to run when you are carrying scissors. What makes it risky?' The first of these two examples reinforces two misunderstandings:

- the synonymity of risk and danger;
- the idea that objects can have intentions (see Williams et al. 1989b; Coombes 1991).

The second example provides the teacher with an opportunity to introduce or reinforce the role of personal responsibility in managing a risk.

If children associate risk with sudden and severe outcomes, then we must tackle this construction of meaning before we link smoking or drug use to the concept of risk. A child experimenting with smoking, who 'knows' smoking is risky, may be expecting a dreadful experience. When this does not occur they may experience a rise in self-esteem and a greater sense of personal control at

Table 8.1 The perceptions of risk of children of primary school age compared with those of adults, both determined using the 'draw and write' technique

Features of an immature perception of risk	Features of a mature perception of risk
immediate, short-term outcome	awareness of long-term consequences
no perception of long-term outcomes	awareness of cumulative risk
high probability of harm to self	risks with both high and low probability depicted
very severe outcomes	a range of outcomes depicted
disproportionate lack of awareness of everyday hazards	awareness of everyday hazards
simplistic cause and effect	multiple cause and effect scenarios
little or no inclusion of danger to others	concern for the safety of others, as well as self
risk associated with misbehaviour, revealing fear of authority	fear of the actions of others, especially as a result of crime
little sense of personal control	strong sense of personal control
little awareness of peer influence on personal behaviour	high awareness of peer influence on personal behaviour

having overcome this challenge. If the challenge is also against authority, the sense of satisfaction may be even greater.

If children are unaware of the impact of their behaviour on the safety of others, and are also unaware of the potential impact of others on their own behaviour, then drugs education should address these issues. Relationship skills should be at the heart of any health education programme, and the impact of relationships in the specific context of illegal and legal drugs use should be made explicit to the pupils through role play and discussion of scenarios involving hazard recognition, risk assessment and risk management.

Risk as a part of normal behaviour
We must recognize that risk taking is a normal part of human behaviour. If we were not risk takers we would not learn to crawl away from our mothers, to walk or climb stairs. There are evolutionary advantages to the risk taker in obtaining food, shelter, a mate. Risk education would allow drugs education to take a more positive approach. The promotion of a realistic sense of one's ability to be in control and to behave effectively in a range of situations would be enhanced by opportunities to take part in activities which *feel* risky but where the level of risk is controlled.

This is the basis of many Outward Bound courses for young people. Planned opportunities for risk-taking for young people don't all need to be physical either. Anyone who has performed in the school play or assembly will know this. Global Rock Challenge, recently introduced into the UK, invites young people to compose, choreograph and perform their own rock music and offers

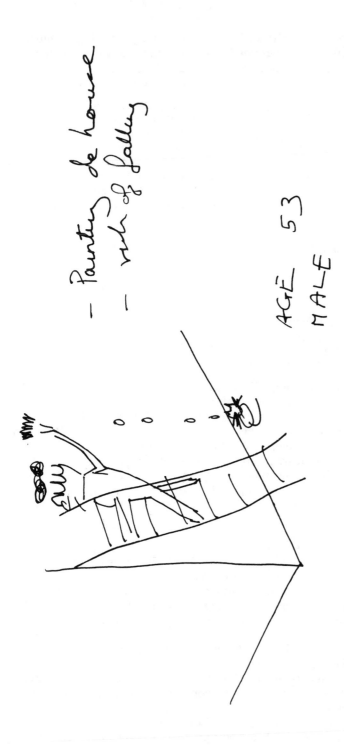

Figure 8.3 Adult perceptions of risk indicate an awareness of everyday hazards

a similarly challenging experience. Young people must be non-smokers for the duration of the preparation and performances, and such is the attraction of the event that regular smokers have been known to give up to be allowed to take part. At a recent event in Hampshire the only people not cheering and applauding at the end were the adults who could not sit through the whole smoke-free evening without slipping out for a cigarette!

Planning a spiral curriculum

While it is important to know where learners are starting from, we should also know where we are planning to take them, and why. Knowing what an adult perception of risk is will help us to plan a spiral curriculum, one which will help young people develop their understanding using appropriate activity, and appropriate language. A curriculum which includes drugs education for 11-year-old pupils should be building on previous work on:

- what makes people feel good and not so good (with nursery aged pupils);
- the role of medicines in preventing illness (with 5- to 6-year-old pupils);
- how bodies deal with excess (with 8-year-old pupils).

Tackling issues such as addiction and the reasons some drugs are illegal or harmful if misused will be more difficult, more frightening without a spiral approach to the curriculum.

Schools as health-promoting organizations

Finally, as Tones and Tilford (1994) have asserted, health information and health-related skills are not sufficient to promote health and well-being. Institutions must provide opportunities for pupils to make choices and to take responsibility. These authors suggest that healthy public policy can amplify the impact of health education: Health promotion = health education × healthy public policy. In a school this may be restated as: Promoting the health of the children, staff and families = a spiral curriculum developing knowledge, understanding, skill and personal responsibility, based on starting where people are × a whole school policy, supported by an ethos where policy is revealed in day-to-day practice in the classroom and within the community.

This is the basis for the health promoting school and reminds us that, no matter how good our curriculum programme, we are likely to fail if we do not also have effective, relevant policies which are known and implemented by all those who work with the children in this context. This includes lunch-time supervisors, visiting police officers, the school nurse and the teachers. Drugs education must be part, then, of a whole-school approach to health education.

'GETTING IT RIGHT' IN HAMPSHIRE

There is some evidence that curriculum programmes, supported by professionals within the community, can help children towards a more mature perception of risk. Pupils in Hampshire schools have been taking part in the Getting it Right Project run by Hampshire Constabulary in co-operation with the Local Education Authority. Twenty-four officers were trained specifically to work with primary school children and their teachers to deliver a programme of education focused on accident reduction, crime prevention and preventing the misuse of substances. A study using the 'draw and write' technique explored the perceptions of risk of 9- to 10-year-old pupils before and after an eighteen-month trial period, and compared these with the perceptions of pupils in Dorset schools who had no similar police liaison scheme.

The study revealed that pupil's perceptions of risk matured over the eighteen-month period in both control and intervention groups. Progress towards a more mature understanding of risk was greater and more consistent amongst pupils in schools involved with the Getting it Right Project. The full details of this study are the subject of a report to Hampshire Constabulary.

The results of the evaluation study in Hampshire suggest that if we were to take seriously the issue of risk education, scattered as it is throughout the curriculum, delivered as it is by a wide range of professionals, and co-ordinate this within a whole-school approach to health education we might address some of the unresolved problems of drugs education in the 1990s and beyond.

NOTE

1. Some of the work described in this chapter forms part of reports commissioned by the Royal Society for the Prevention of Accidents (RoSPA) and Hampshire Constabulary.

REFERENCES

Aggleton, P. (1995) *Health Promotion and Young People: A report to the HEA*. London: Health Education Research Unit, Institute of Education, University of London.

Baric, L. (1996) *Health Promotion and Health Education: Handbook for Students and Practitioners*. Altrincham: Barns Publications.

Coombes, G. (1991) *You can't Watch Them 24 Hours a Day*. London: CAPT, HEA, Health Education Board for Scotland, Community Education Development Centre and Northern Ireland Department of Health and Social Services.

Englander, T., Farago, F., Slovic, P. and Fischhoff, B. (1986) A comparative analysis of risk perception in Hungary and the United States. *Social Behaviour*, **1**, 55–6.

Gibbons, F.X., Helweg Larsen, M. and Gerrard, M. (1995) Prevalence estimates and adolescent risk taking behaviour: cross cultural differences in social influence. *Journal of Applied Psychology*, **80**(1), 107–21.

Hopson, B. and Scally, M. (1981) *Lifeskills Teaching*. London: McGraw-Hill.

Hughes, B., Wetton, N., Collins, M. and Newton Bishop, J. (1996) Health education about sun and skin cancer: language ideas and perceptions of young children. *British Journal of Dermatology*, **134**, 412–17.

McWhirter, J. (1993) A teenager's view of puberty. *Health Education*, May, 9–11.

McWhirter, J. and Wetton, N. (1994) Children's perceptions of risk. *British Journal of Health and Safety* **10**, 21–9. Birmingham: British Health and Safety Society.

Mortimer, F. (1997) Adult perceptions of risk. MSc dissertation, University of Southampton.

Oakley, A., Bendelow, G., Barnes, J., Buchanan, M. and Husain, O.A.N. (1995) Health and cancer prevention: knowledge and beliefs of children and young people. *British Medical Journal*, **310**, 1029–33.

O'Connor, L., Best, D.W., Best, R.M. and Rowley, J. (1997) *Young People, Drugs and Drugs Education: Missed Opportunities.* Report of a collaborative research into three London Boroughs: Merton, Sutton and Wandsworth. London: Roehampton Institute.

Porcellato, L., Dugdil, L., Springett, J. and Sanderson, F. (1996) *Attitudes, Beliefs and Smoking Behaviour in Liverpool Primary School Children: An Interim Research Report.* Liverpool: Institute for Health, Liverpool John Moores University.

Slovic, P., Fischoff, B. and Lichtenstein, S. (1981) Perceived risk: psychological factors and social implications. *Proceedings of the Royal Society of London*, **376**, 17–34. London: Royal Society.

Tones, K. and Tilford, S. (1994) *Health Education: Effectiveness, Efficiency and Equity*, second edition. London: Chapman & Hall.

Wetton, N. (1992) Primary school children and the world of drugs. In Evans, R. and O'Connor, L. (eds) *Drug Abuse and Misuse: Developing Educational Strategies in Partnership*, Roehampton Institiute Occasional Papers No. 1. London: David Fulton.

Wetton, N. and McWhirter, J.M. (1998) Image based curriculum development in health education. In Prosser, J. (ed.) *Image Based Research: A Source Book for Qualitative Researchers*. Brighton: Falmer Press.

Williams, T., Wetton, N. and Moon, A. (1989a) *A Picture of Health*. London: Health Education Authority.

Williams, T., Wetton, N. and Moon, A. (1989b) *A Weigh In: Five Key Areas of Health Education*. London: Health Education Authority.

CHAPTER 9

Training the drugs educators: quality assurance for schools

Vivienne Evans

INTRODUCTION

For many teachers drugs education is fraught with difficulties. These difficulties are personal, organizational and related to the curriculum.

Drugs education is a desirable component of the curriculum, not a requirement. This means that its status in schools, despite the guidelines outlined in *Drug Prevention and Schools* (Circular 4/95, Department for Education, 1995), is often low in terms of teacher and pupil perception. As with all Personal, Social and Health Education – into which curriculum slot drugs education is fitted in most schools – it does not attract a high priority because it is not examined, there are no written tests or homework assignments and the classroom methodologies of group work and discussion tasks are viewed as the 'underbelly' of the curriculum, rather than the 'real stuff' which should be going on in 'proper subjects'.

On an organizational level, this low status is confirmed. Drugs education is often delivered by reluctant, non-specialist teachers in what is described as 'tutor' time but in reality often means a few minutes in the morning when administrative details have to be communicated to pupils. On a personal level this translates into the way teachers feel about what they are asked to do. The lack of training produces a lack of confidence and competence (see for example Ofsted 1997). Yet the *issue* of drugs is currently hugely important and the expectation for it to be tackled in schools, from a curriculum policy and organizational dimension, is very high (*Tackling Drugs Together*, White Paper 1995).

Many teachers believe that to 'teach' drugs education you have to know the facts, and that, because the drug culture is predominantly a youth culture, young people know more about it than they do. These assumptions obviously contain some element of truth but they lead to a far more dangerous conviction that teachers themselves are unable to 'teach' about drugs. Because there is an organizational expectation for drugs education to be delivered, this in turn leads to the use of representatives from external agencies – often believed to be 'experts' who visit the classroom to undertake this element.

Teachers often see themselves as unskilled in this area of work because of the mistaken belief that drug education is all about imparting knowledge; the principles and practice of sound personal and social education are abandoned (TACADE/London Drug Policy Forum 1997). Yet evidence gained from evaluation of drugs education programmes indicate the need for knowledge-based approaches to be supported by interactive methods and address perceptions and values (Coggans and Watson 1995).

TRAINING FOR TEACHERS IN DRUGS EDUCATION: QUALITY STANDARDS

In order to address the generally patchy provision of drugs education, quality standards need to apply to the training which drugs educators receive. In schools they need to develop internal expertise to equip them to offer effective classroom practice and to formulate and implement drugs policies. The Department for Education and Employment endorses this view: 'The main focus of teacher training on drug prevention must ... be appropriate in-service training for teachers' (*Drug Prevention and Schools*, Circular 4/95, Department for Education). In an ideal world every practitioner who was expected to deliver drugs education, and every manager who was expected to develop and implement a drugs policy, would experience appropriate training in this area. In the current climate, despite Department for Education and Employment financial incentives, this is not possible. Money and human resources are limited. Furthermore, drugs education holds a nebulous place in the Science National Curriculum. The basic framework is outlined, but this does not allow for adequate resources to be allocated to this area within either initial teacher education or in-service provision (O'Connor 1995).

In practical terms this means that drugs education courses available to teachers are usually bought in by the school or local authority from an external agency. On local-authority-based courses, which are attended by teachers from a range of schools, the expectation is usually that the delegated teacher goes back to school to disseminate the course content to colleagues. This kind of cascade model of training is theoretically a good one, but is often fraught with difficulty and does not necessarily ensure high-quality drugs education implementation. Cascade training, by its very nature, dissipates the calibre of the original training. It relies on several assumptions: that the teacher attending the course possesses the training skills to replicate the training experience; that course content can be passed on via handouts and leaflets – information about drugs for example – and that the course is knowledge-based. This may be true in some cases, and, in terms of teachers learning about local drug patterns, prevalence and recognition, a knowledge-based, 'give 'em the facts' style of course may achieve expected outcomes. However, this does not sufficiently address teachers' confidence and capability to deliver broad-based, interactive drugs education (O'Connor 1995).

Financial constraints also determine the style and type of courses available for drugs educators. The courses tend to be of one day's duration. Although one-day courses can and should deliver the most important quality standard – that of improving the quality of practice – it is time to promote the requirement for courses which provide a professional qualification or contribute to a qualification. This implies that courses should be of standard duration to comply with the standards of an accrediting institution, and should include written work and a self-reporting element which requires the drugs educator to reflect on professional practice.

Quality standards should apply to the drugs education courses which are available to teachers. Because of the perceived lack of expertise within the teaching profession in the drugs area, a variety of agencies and professional groups act as providers. How can purchasers ensure that they are buying high-quality experiences for the course participants?

The kind of questions which are posed to visitors to classrooms from external agencies serve as a starting point. Shared values, for example, are key. But beyond this, unless quality standards are set out by the agency, there is no guarantee that the training experience will be valid and worthwhile (TACADE/London Drug Policy Forum 1997).

KEY PRINCIPLES

The following key principles could be used as a basis for quality assurance.

Assessment of participants' needs

To be effective, training courses should meet the needs of the participants. By implication this means that, in order to promote best practice, training providers should ensure that an assessment of needs takes place prior to the contracting of the training provider. To achieve this, schools could conduct brief needs assessments by issuing questionnaires or holding focus group interviews with staff members. In practical terms this takes time and resources, and the reality is that schools may well respond to 'gut reactions' and needs based on informal discussions and perceptions. These perceptions may well be that what they primarily need in a 'drugs education course' is information, rather than a training experience which will equip them to deliver drugs education within the context of personal and social education, and the learning methodologies which support this approach.

The DfE Circular supports this rather limited view by indicating that confidence to teach drugs education is primarily inspired by knowing the facts: 'Teachers who are responsible for teaching about drugs or for co-ordinating a school's programme of drug education and drug prevention need to be given the confidence to deliver clear and consistent messages about drugs, and need access to up to date facts about drug misuse.' There is a concession that an awareness of successful teaching approaches is also needed, but this component of a course programme may be marginalized when training is delivered to multi-agency groups.

Targeted recruitment

This is a critical factor, linked to needs assessment. The objectives, and therefore the course programme, should ideally be built around the identified needs of the participants, who should be recruited to ensure appropriateness and capacity for implementation. A course programme which concentrates on classroom practice, for example, is not as appropriate for senior managers in schools as it is for practitioners. A course programme which focuses on policy development is not as appropriate for practitioners as it is for managers.

This leads to the issue of multi-disciplinary training. By its very nature, training people from different backgrounds and professions is restricted because it cannot address specific needs. It can only meet limited objectives, and on drugs education courses those objectives will primarily be concerned with delivering facts and information about drugs, and with sharing expertise. The *concept* of bringing people from different perceptions and experiences together to share a training course is believed to be beneficial because it encourages the exchange of good practice and helps increase participants' local contacts and information. This in turn can widen participants' perceptions, views and attitudes. The Department for Education advice encourages this approach: 'Where general training is being provided about drugs and young people it can be particularly valuable for teaching staff to train alongside other professionals such as school nurses, the police, health and social services personnel, youth workers and staff from specialist drug prevention agencies.'

Recruitment and planning linked to multi-disciplinary consensus

High-quality multi-disciplinary training does and can exist but objectives must be clear and expectations targeted at what is achievable and relevant for this type of course. The issue of recruitment is also linked to that of participants' expectations and the logistical requirements of planning. It is the experience of many trainers that they arrive to tutor a course only to find that the participants' expectations are at odds with those stated on the course programme. This usually occurs because communication has broken down between purchaser and provider, so either the participants do not possess a programme or the one they have, written by the purchaser, is not compatible with that written by the provider. It is not uncommon for the participants to expect to receive, for example, information about how to spot a drug and a drug taker and to discover that the course is designed to consider the curriculum implications of drugs education or the development of a school drugs policy. All this leads to frustrated and often antagonistic course members.

It is thus vital that the training provider is equipped with sufficient information about the training needs of the participants and the target group, so an appropriate course programme can be written, agreed by the purchaser and communicated to the participants. By the same token, purchasers need to ensure that the training provider requests some indication of training needs and designs a programme which meets those needs. Promoting quality in drugs education training is a two-way, negotiated process.

In order to maintain quality, the provider agency needs to request certain practical information which will help shape the framework of the course and the programme. How many participants are to attend the course, for example? More than about thirty can be unmanageable for an experiential course, and more than one trainer may be needed. Is the size of the training room adequate to accommodate the participants and allow for group work sessions? Practical considerations like these can dictate course methodology and must be discussed by providers and purchasers in order to ensure quality.

Clear objectives and course programmes which attempt to achieve them

Needs assessment, targeting and recruitment shape the objectives, learning outcomes and course programme. Programmes should be designed to achieve the objectives and learning outcomes by the use of appropriate methods. The methods will reflect the underlying educational philosophy of the provider agency and to a certain extent will shape the framework of the course.

If a course is to use experiential, active methodologies the trainer must build a relatively safe learning environment. This can be achieved by ensuring that the whole group size is not large, and by using a variety of activities which promote a sense of group coherence. On one-day courses, which is all most purchasers of drugs education courses can afford, this process is vital but must be brief. Otherwise participants tend not to appreciate its value. Some activities to set ground rules, to determine expectations and outline learning outcomes should be required elements of a largely experiential course.

Experiential methods are not, *per se*, requirements which determine quality. A variety of methods and the ability of the trainer to be flexible in adjusting to meet specific needs and situations is necessary. Some input from the trainer is often necessary to promote credibility and to offer information. Although, for example, facts about drugs can be effectively communicated and learned through methods like quizzes and card games, the trainer will need a sound knowledge about drugs in order to answer questions during the feedback session. If trainers are not familiar with drug-specific content, they will need to co-train with someone who is, or restrict the information session to an input given by an 'expert'.

The use of highly skilled and credible trainers

It is perhaps self-evident that the person who leads a drugs education course needs to possess a range of group leadership and management skills. These skills include the ability to communicate, to listen, to take feedback critically and imaginatively, to value the contributions of everyone in the group and to create a purposeful working environment in a short space of time. In order to have credibility with course participants, it is also essential for the trainer to have recognized experience and qualifications relevant to the task in hand.

However, if a course is to achieve the objective of affecting practice – of empowering participants to take action as a result of attendance – then it must be led by a trainer who motivates and inspires confidence rather than by someone who gives the impression of being omnipotent. This is particularly true of cascade models of training. If teachers are expected to go back to school and to disseminate the initial training experience, they must feel assured of their abilities.

The inclusion of action planning in the course programme

In order for participants to be able to do more as a result of the course – to be more highly skilled themselves and thus to improve the quality of the 'service to clients' – a structured action planning session should be included in the course programme. This element also has the potential of helping to meet a wide variety of expectations which may well be present on a multi-disciplinary course. Police officers, for example, will need to be able to change and enhance their current practice, which will be different to the current practice of teachers. Course participants should be encouraged to develop an action plan which states intended outcomes, specifies targets, and defines and identifies organizational roles and responsibilities.

The importance and inclusion of evaluation

The extent to which a course fulfils its objectives will partly be answered by some kind of evaluation. On many one-day courses all that this means in practice is that participants fill in an evaluation form. To promote quality standards in training the evaluation is crucial if, and only if, it informs the future development of that training. Trainers must be clear about the questions they wish to be answered. For example, do they want to know about their own skills as a trainer; do they want to know if course participants' expectations have been met – and were these expectations realistic in the first place; do they need to know how far participants believe the course experience will impact on their current practice; do they need to know how the course programme might be improved; do they need to know how far the learning objectives have been met? Trainers thus need to be clear about what they want their evaluation to discover and to design appropriate evaluation strategies. In terms of quality it is important to attempt to find out more than the *feelings* which participants have about the course; an attempt to evaluate changes in practice, in abilities and skills should be attempted. In order for this to have real validity, some kind of long-term evaluation is needed which will demonstrate evidence of impact (where this exists). Again, resources are limited for this kind of study and there tends to be a focus on short-term outcome evaluation, rather than an appraisal of the implementation factors which need to be in place before the effectiveness of a drugs education programme can be assessed (Dobson and Wright/TACADE 1995).

THE NEED FOR QUALITY STANDARDS

Nationally agreed quality standards for the training of drugs educators do not exist. There is clearly a need. TACADE's work in conducting drug training audits in the past has used quality standards developed from existing criteria set by national professional bodies. The criteria has thus been based on the training needs of individual professional groups, rather than those of drugs educators. Given the differing needs of different professional groups, and the need to use training as the wherewithal to improve professional practice, there is an urgent need to develop quality standards in the training of drugs educators.

In the development of quality standards it is important to take into account the needs of providers, consumers and the professional organization within which drugs educators work. Demonstrating a commitment to drugs training and assigning it as a priority is the role and responsibility of the professional organization; identifying training needs and negotiating a contract for training which meets these needs is largely the responsibility of the purchaser; delivering a quality experience to the consumer is the responsibility of the individual trainer or training agency.

ACCREDITED QUALIFICATIONS

If quality standards should be developed, so should the opportunities for drugs educators to achieve a recognized qualification in drugs education. Training should be accredited, which would afford it high status, and consist of key elements which combine theory with practice. Courses which are underpinned by research into best practice, and given credibility through nationally recognized criteria, are the best way forward. They must be subjected to external objective tests and fit within a recognized system of qualifications. Courses could well be set up as multi-disciplinary as long as a high level of practical implementation (for example of classroom practice or drugs policy development in the school context) were included, together with opportunities for participants to reflect on and evaluate their practice. Flexible packages should be developed which allow partnerships between provider agencies and academic institutions to offer accredited courses; these may not necessarily be taught in the traditional way. Open and distance learning should be considered, along with the use of modern technology as learning tools.

Examples of accredited multi-disciplinary training already exist. A Home Office evaluation was in 1997 being undertaken of the degree-level Certificate in Drugs Prevention and Education – a collaborative effort between the North West London Drugs Prevention Initiative Team and Roehampton Institute London. At present TACADE is working with Barnsley Education Authority to establish an accredited course for teachers and related professionals which will lead to a nationally recognized qualification within a competency-based framework. This project is funded by the Department for Education and Employment GEST budget and the LEA.

In the meantime effective training is the great need of many professionals in the education sphere. So often it is marginalized and under-resourced. What most teachers say on their evaluation forms at the conclusion of a day's drugs education training course is that they need more training. Only when training for drugs educators is accredited, standardized and afforded high status will quality of training and thus consistently improved practice be assured.

REFERENCES

Advisory Council on the Misuse of Drugs, Home Office (1993) *Drug Education in Schools: The Need for New Impetus.* London: HMSO.

Alcohol Concern (undated) *A National Alcohol Training Strategy.* London: Alcohol Concern.

Coggans, N. and Watson, J. (1995) *Drug Education: Approaches, Effectiveness and Implications for Delivery.* Health Education Board for Scotland.

Department for Education (1995) *Drug Prevention and Schools.* Circular 4/95. London: DfE.

Dobson, B.E. and Wright, L. /TACADE (1995) *The Effective Implementation of Drug Education in 5 European Countries.* Brussels: European Commission.

O'Connor, L. (1991) Health education: feeling the squeeze. *Education and Health,* **9**(2), 28–31.

O'Connor, L. (1995) Accrediting health education. *ASHEC News,* **9**.

Office For Standards in Education (1997) *Drug Education in Schools.* London: HMSO.

TACADE (1993) *A Review of Alcohol and Drug Training in Nottinghamshire.* Report to the Nottingham Drug Training Audit Group. Salford: TACADE.

TACADE (1994) *Skills for Life: A Whole School Approach to Personal and Social Development.* Salford: TACADE.

TACADE and London Drug Policy Forum (1996) *Making the Most of Visitors: The Use of Outside Agencies in School Drug Education.* Salford: TACADE/ LGDF.

White Paper (1995) *Tackling Drugs Together: A Strategy for England, 1995–1998.* CMD 2846. London: HMSO.

CHAPTER 10

Reaching out to young people: informal settings and drugs education

Colin Chapman

Current public concerns 'stoked up' by the media about young people and drugs are based on a succession of surveys and polls conducted among teenagers. They indicate increasing levels of drug use but do not explain the role and purpose of drugs in the social world of young people from different backgrounds, cultures and abilities. Such statistics explain neither why the majority do not use illicit substances but perhaps mimic their elders by indulging in the more conventional pleasures of smoking and drinking, nor why a further minority do not indulge in any drug consumption. These statistics, rather than encouraging reasonable debate and discussion with young people, tend to fuel ill-judged campaigns that are warmly endorsed by those who have rejected illegal drugs but are largely ignored by the 'using group', unimpressed by what they see as propaganda, scoffing at the hypocrisy of it all, set against the unbridled promotion of alcohol and tobacco, which the increasingly sophisticated young drug users see as the substances that have damaged so many in their parents' generation.

The focus of information in education programmes has also been questioned. While this can be assessed as a way of improving knowledge, without a context where young people can talk over their concerns and debate the issues, little lasting value will be achieved by providing information alone.

De Haes (1987) concluded that the success of education and prevention initiatives will not be realized until there is a more complete understanding between the substance, the individual user and the social cultural context in which use occurs. We need then to look at some in-depth research among groups of young people to get a handle on the place, or lack of it, of drugs in the lives of young people. What is the place and meaning of drugs in their lives, and how can this help us in determining ways in which we can engage young people about the issues? Understanding the function of drugs in the lives of adolescents is not of course the whole story. Those engaged with drugs education, whether it be peer educators, teachers or youth workers, will want to raise matters that young people had not considered. This would be part of a negotiated approach to the subject.

So what are young people saying about the importance of drugs to them?

Clearly it cannot be wrapped and boxed in generalizations, and drugs will mean different things at different times to young people, we know that all are exposed to some degree.

Much has been made of a distinctive youth culture, and there is no doubt that the postwar period has revealed the phenomenon of youth, which featured some notorious subcultural groupings ranging from 'hippies' and 'punks' to 'mods' and 'rockers'. All that remains known from the subcultural era is the nostalgic recreations in specialist shops. The demise of such groups tends to support the theory that young people are largely conventional. This was noted by the distinguished American sociologist Talcott Parsons (see Stewart 1992), who in the 1950s wrote that 'young people had only a vague antipathy towards the adult world and seemed more concerned with having a good time and wanting to appear physically attractive as a source of peer group status'. He also identified irresponsibility and the prevalence of sport as an avenue of achievement (in contrast to adult occupational achievement). Stewart (1992) provided further evidence from market research of the essentially conventional attitudes of young people. This revealed that young people would like to be seen as sensible and responsible, sensitive, caring, and intelligent. These are not the qualities the media likes to dwell on.

If we turn to research which has gone some way to unmask the drug scene among youth, we find that a number of conclusions have been reached which should be taken into account when considering promising directions for drugs education programmes, whether in formal or informal settings. First, the perception of young people is one of drugs simply being around, something that is just there, not something that is central or dominates their lives in any particular way (Hirst and McCamley-Finney 1994).

One peer education project, Youth Link Wales, estimates that each young person has at least forty friends and acquaintances, and it is within this group that drugs are obtained rather than offered. So often the question asked in market research amongst young people is 'when were you offered drugs?' Also found in a study amongst London teenagers was the fact that drug use was not central to their lives but an accepted part of leisure activity (Power *et al.* 1996). Coffield and Gofton (1994) argue that young people approach soft drugs in the same rational and matter-of-fact way that they deal with other consumer goods. In support, Stewart (1992) pointed to the consumption ethic as a governing factor in young people's lives. Hirst and McCamley-Finney (1994) found in their research among Sheffield teenagers that drugs are selected with financial restrictions in mind, and again Coffield and Gofton (1994) also highlight costs as a determinate of choice: 'certain kinds of drug taking then may be more appropriately viewed as a rational response to the costs involved in taking comparable legal drugs?' Coffield and Gofton (1994) extend their argument, stressing that particular types of drink and drugs are used by young people to try out different identities, to explore various aspects of themselves which do not find expression elsewhere, to dramatize an area of their otherwise humdrum lives, to show membership of a particular group or to manifest socially important characteristics (maturity, taste, power, sexual attractiveness and even a particular philosophical outlook). The problems identified by young people in the Sheffield study are attributed to the action of others in response to their drug taking, such as exclusion from school, being turned out of youth centres, panic in hostels and residential care, as well as parents calling helplines and parents' threats to kill them. These reactions are perceived by the young people as being based on inaccurate information, misunderstandings and a failure to communicate. This is important, as young people consistently talk of turning in the first instance to parents, and maybe other friendly adults, for help and support (O'Connor *et al.* 1997).

Some commentators point to the normalization of illicit drug use among young people (Parker *et al.* 1995). In contrast, other research has reported that young people in general do not experience illicit drug use on a 'normal' basis (O'Connor *et al.* 1997). However, where drug use is prevalent there will be a considerable number of young people who will not have used drugs, and have come to the conclusion through witnessing the impact of drugs on peers that it is foolish because of the health implications, fear of addiction and loss of control, cost, damage to relationships with peers and parents, and particularly the association between drug use and crime and violence (Shiner and Newburn 1996).

EXPERIENCES OF DRUGS EDUCATION

Young people in studies reviewed were critical of drugs education, if they had received it: they described it as often being late and introduced inappropriately. One described it as 'just blurted out, all the bad stuff, to two hundred kids in assembly' (Shiner and Newburn 1996). In the studies considered, young people were particularly responsive to the researchers who took an interest in them and validated their views (O'Connor *et al.* 1997).

Shiner and Newburn (1996) distinguished three dimensions relating to the credibility of a drugs education programme. These were: person-based credibility arising from the educators' personal characteristics, for example age, sex or ethnic origin; experience-based credibility, arising from the educators' experience as perceived by the audience, for example drug misuse, contact with the criminal justice system or bereavement; and message-based credibility, arising from what the educator is saying and the way they are saying it.

The crucial position of the facilitator in any drugs education programme cannot be overemphasized. It has perhaps been overlooked in recent developments in drugs education, which to some extent has been resource-led or programme-led, rather than person-led, with packs often lavishly produced as the 'mother' of all resources, designed to cover all eventualities. At one glittering launch the remark was made, 'Thank God it has arrived'. Realistically, off-the-shelf packages, no matter how carefully produced and originally designed, tend to have similar contents and can be a block to talking with young people, with the energy going into getting through the programme. There is an added pressure in this era of 'outcomes and short-term fundings' to come up with some nicely targeted innovative programmes that systematically address an issue such as drugs. Drug use cannot be boxed, labelled and simply dealt with, yet in the domain of young peoples' lives it may be the intervention of a sympathetic adult or older peer that is crucial in providing the necessary support at a particular time (O'Connor 1995). The author has not forgotten advocating an interactive approach to a group of teachers on one occasion, when one interjected that they felt that, without denouncing the value of discussion, it was appropriate to speak to the class directly on occasions on such issues as the dangers of drugs. My argument was that the teacher concerned had sufficient credibility to be heard by the young people. Perhaps we should not be making a special thing about drugs education, merging it in with other sensitive issues and having a flexible and wide-ranging approach, which is planned but sometimes spontaneous and timely. The first practical approach that will be discussed may seem blindingly obvious, but in the busy schedules of professional youth workers, teachers and others there is sometimes not the time to go out of their way to talk with young people, and the danger is always, in formal and informal settings, that encounters occur when some disciplinary issue arises.

COMMUNICATING ON DRUG ISSUES: TAKING OPPORTUNITIES

When the Health Education Authority commissioned health education materials for older teenagers published as *The Health Action Pack* (1987), research confirmed the value of talking as a means of health education (Chamberlain 1987). Talking with, as opposed to talking to or at, conveys an image of conversation between peers or equals. Here lies the freedom to choose when or if an exchange should begin, how it may be continued and when and how it may be ended. The talking that goes on outside the formal educational programme is by nature not so constrained, so that both parties given an acceptance of confidentiality, can be free to set an agenda that is more finely attuned to needs. In fact many youth workers would say that their best work is conducted on a trip out in the minibus, or leaning up against the bar in the club with a few youngsters who just want to stand around and test out ideas and thoughts. One youth worker commented that he thought the most important thing was that you should be starting with the young people themselves. We as adults can come up with an agenda for them but you need to talk to them. The youth worker interviewed was keen to play up the value of exchanging conversation, saying that 'some people think that when they are chatting it is not worthwhile, but it is difficult to justify, I think it's very valuable'. The author can recall as a youth work trainee spending time practising talking with young people, listening to their language and their views, trying to get a feel for their thinking as well as learning to chip in with suitable interjections which were not seen as nosy or talking down, but trying to be open and genuine with them.

The importance of treating young people's views, experiences and ideas with respect cannot be overemphasized: they are sometimes not given credit for what they know and understand. Young people do appreciate the opportunity to talk things over, but adults do find it difficult and often the mood of the moment or the situation does not allow conversations to take place. If no cues are offered it may be better to wait for an opportunity to occur some other time. Chance conversations which are be a matter of routine for the worker may be highly valued for the young person, and reflected back perhaps years later as a crucial point of support when at the time it did not seem so significant.

When at last an opportunity arose to talk with a young person who had previously only managed a grunt or abusive remark, the writer found it was well worth pursuing, even though there may have been a riot going in another section of the club! In the HEA research many staff said that they did have problems coping with young people and that sometimes they did not want to know and had made up their own minds. As one worker commented, 'When we were coming back one day in the minibus they were talking about getting paralytic, I didn't say anything, I did not want to intrude.' This poses difficult issues for workers in settings which are voluntary, unlike the compulsory school setting.

Sometimes the collective desire of young people to just talk can be channelled into a 'talking' group. One youth club harnessed and processed this verbal energy into a weekly think tank. Using a separate room in the centre, with an old standard lamp providing some subdued lighting and refreshments available, the session began with the members determining the agenda. The air was rich with expletives but the discussion was compelling and chaotic. With the worker acting more like a ringmaster than a facilitator, young people were able to voice their ideas, opinions and experiences in ways they had previously been unable to do (Chapman 1995). The value of tapping into young people's knowledge, insights and experiences cannot be overemphasized in the process of drugs education (O'Connor et al. 1997).

TACKLING DRUGS IN A DYNAMIC WAY AND PROVIDING ALTERNATIVES

In informal settings drugs education may occur not as a separate planned event but in response to situations that arise. It may be dealt with confrontationally but may also have the potential for creative work to arise. At one centre where the author worked, the premises had become a focus for drug use, mainly the consumption of and dealing in cannabis. It was clear that decisive action had to be taken to protect staff and members, prevent a police raid and give those involved a choice regarding their continued membership of the club. The 'crunch' came when an organized drug dealing operation was discovered in the television room. Action was subsequently taken, and after consultation with the club members along the lines that it was not possible for the organization to function as a safe place for staff to work or young people to meet unless drug dealing and drug consumption stopped, full co-operation of the members was achieved. It was the core group in the club that were involved in the drug dealing operation: it was agreed to put a simple notice up saying, 'Soft and hard drugs are banned by law, the law applies in the club, anyone seen in the club smoking, handling or dealing banned substances will be asked to leave'. This did the trick, and the television room was refurbished and reopened as a music room. This became the centre for creative activity where members learned to play drums and guitar: two of the volunteer leaders who were skilled musicians, and who had become exasperated by the time spent in patrolling the club to keep the level of drug use under control, were involved in this project.

In a report made to the management committee the comment was made 'in a climate of widespread drug abuse all we can do is stick to our guns, be firm in the club and in our attitudes and expectations, without getting depressed about the use of drugs, as well as challenging those using without alienating them to the point where they become unreachable'. We could find some humour in the situation: it's a long road, and there are many 'pot' holes, if you will excuse the pun.

In another setting (Gordon 1986) a worker was concerned about certain elements of the current lifestyle of a group of young men which included glue sniffing, getting drunk and hanging around bus shelters. The worker considered these activities undesirable and wanted to offer the group alternatives. He considered that they were not beyond his reach and were susceptible to his influence and in his words 'capable of stepping out of the "dossing" syndrome'. This particular group were interested in music and were in a band already but needed somewhere to practice. There was a discussion about recording, and the worker indicated that a grant could be applied for from a national trust to purchase a portable studio. It initially sounded an impossible target, obtaining a substantial amount of money for their recording equipment. The first goal set by the worker was obtaining a four-track tape recorder to enable them to get immediate hands-on experience. The community arts project was also involved for three months while the application was being processed. The worker reflected that it was a gamble as it might not have worked, and the young people may not have latched on to this goal; but they did and it worked.

This sounds like a fairly routine piece of youth work, but the principle is most important because it is this type of intervention that is more likely to impact on the immediate behaviour of a group of young people at risk: the role of the supportive adult is crucial to the success of the intervention.

PEER EDUCATION

Peer education has developed out of participative approaches to social education. Central to good youth work practice over the years has been the youth council and active member representation on youth club management committees. Peer education has been described as young people being involved in teaching, leading or facilitating work amongst groups of young people of near or similar age. The Scottish peer education movement Fast Forward (1993/4) understands peer education to be an approach which empowers young people to work with other young people, drawing on the strength of positive peer pressure by means of appropriate training and support, with young people becoming active players in the educational process rather than passive recipients of a set message. Central to this work is the collaboration between young people and adults.

Most peer education programmes, according to Frankham (1995), are based on four elements. Young people are seen as ready-made experts in communicating with their peers. Young people already talk openly to each other about sensitive issues such as sex and drugs, and in this sense they can be trained to become 'well informed friends, who will incorporate accurate, appropriate, helpful information about drug use into the discussions they have with their friends'. It is also understood that in more structured circumstances peer educators can break through the barriers of trust that adults may not be able to reach when discussing sensitive and personal issues. Young people are very susceptible to influence by their peer group. Natural leaders are perceived, for example, as being able to provide the sort of role models that other young people will aspire to. Lastly, peer education programmers are cost-effective: young people do not come as expensive as your average freelance professional health educator and trainer, although there are cost implications in their training.

Most current literature related to drugs education and prevention work among young people refers to peer-led approaches as a popular means by which drugs education and prevention messages are imparted, and point to the belief that it has proved effective in encouraging knowledge, attitude and behaviour changes in relation to drugs and AIDS (Power *et al.* 1996). Given the fact that it is widely acknowledged by drug agencies and police that young people obtain drugs via friends and relatives rather than persons unknown, it seems productive to provide education within peer groups. Thus key individuals who are opinion leaders in these friendship networks can be engaged as peer educators, 'indigenous advocates to promote harm minimisation and drug prevention' (Power *et al.* 1996). Peer education cannot take place without adult vision, commitment and involvement. Young people have to be recruited and sold the benefits that arise from getting involved in helping their peers and learning new skills and responsibilities. The Fast Forward Project has spent several years developing principles which underpin a work philosophy in involving young people. Their advice is summarized as follows:

Recruitment
- Be clear about the intended role, function and time commitment.
- Accept that there are varied legitimate motivations for volunteering.
- Consider equal opportunities issues; it may be harder to attract young men than young women.
- Don't underplay the challenge of undertaking difficult tasks: they may be an attraction.
- Recruit pairs or friendship groups as well as individuals.

Deployment
- Ensure that appropriate support (moral, administrative and practical) is offered.
- Offer relevant negotiated training.
- Clarify the role of adults involved.
- Always build confidence.
- Address issues relating to power, who makes decisions and who is accountable.
- Recognize and make use of the natural dynamics of the group work process.
- Ensure that volunteers get a personal 'pay-off': this is rarely financial and needs to be different for each individual.
- Beware of 'cloning' where young people simply take on the style and the approach of adult trainers.

Moving On
- Beware of the dangers of early 'burn-out' from asking young people to do too much to soon.
- Be clear about how volunteers can leave. There is no shame in wanting to move on.

Like Fast Forward, Youth Link Wales is a peer education organization that also derives its philosophy and practice from the youth service. It is described as a young people's organization about the prevention of substance misuse which includes alcohol, drugs, solvents, HIV and AIDS. Youth Link is run by young people who decide and plan its activities. They acknowledge that there has been limited evaluation about the impact of peer-led education as a drug prevention device, but are clear that, as a result of the programmes conducted, young people have grown in self-worth and have learnt about the issues and acted as 'conduits' for other peers. Young people at Youth Link are seen not as volunteers but as owning the whole process, and are confident that members have become more realistic about their attitudes towards drugs and more skilled at cutting through the media 'hype' that there is towards the issue. They also appear to be more confident about raising drug issues with parents and have recently produced a magazine for parents to create a dialogue within families. They fear that some peer education programmes which are commissioned have unrealistic objectives and are planned in too short a time frame.

Clearly there are considerable dilemmas around any organization that is youth-led: how much support the adults should give and to what extent young people are allowed to make mistakes, as well as what level of intervention is allowed without undermining the work the young people have established. Frankham (1995) remarked in observing peer education on HIV:

> I am not at all surprised peer educators fell into mimicking, if you like the most traditional methods of teaching around. They are likely to be very familiar with people standing at the front of the class telling them what to do, and with so little training and so much anxiety associated with running seminars, such formulaic ways of behaving will come natural to them.

Some of these questions are resolved partly through training, or by establishing a culture that requires sharing and partnership with young people, taking responsibility for supporting and controlling each other (Best *et al.* 1995; Clements and Buczkiewicz 1993).

SCHOOL CONFERENCES FOR YOUNG PEOPLE USING A MULTI-AGENCY PARTNERSHIP IN A LONDON BOROUGH

In one London borough an approach was taken which to some extent was a compromise between the belief that drugs education in schools should be teacher-led and the demands from the school for the involvement of workers from local specialist agencies to take on the responsibility of organizing such education and the principals of peer education.

The situation in the 1980s had become acute, with schools finding increasing difficulty in releasing teachers for training as drugs educators owing to the growing demands of the National Curriculum. Alongside this were the increasing levels of drug taking amongst young people locally. Measures were taken that were not designed to replace existing programmes but to offer a different dimension, bringing in approaches and styles of working familiar in the youth service, based on the principal of actively involving young people in the whole process.

The first conferences involving a whole-year group of young people focused on drugs and sexual health, issues that were on the agenda of the adults involved. Later the agendas were set in consultation with young people and tutors, and the subject areas dramatically broadened. The schools were responsible for the logistics, advertising workshops with brief details about their content. Mostly the conferences lasted half a day or a day, and where possible were held at a local conference or youth centre. The partners in the programme were the drug and alcohol service, youth and community service and the Health Authority, with the youth service providing the majority of facilitators drawn from the part-time youth work team. While not exactly peers, they were certainly, in age terms, in the range of the young people who participated in the workshops. Older people were not excluded, and where they had specialist knowledge and skills and a willingness to work in a participative way they were welcomed into the conference teams.

With some year groups over 280, a considerable number of workshops had to be planned for the group numbers to be kept below 15. It is worth re-emphasizing the value of organizing such events away from the school: it is easier for young people to behave differently in a situation that would normally be associated with their leisure time. There was also relaxation over dress, flexibility of hours (no school bells) and tea and coffee breaks, together with attractive and nutritional lunches. The older the year group the wider the range of issues identified, including, stress, racism, relationships, body image, women's health, welfare issues at college or university, acupuncture, the Alexander Technique, first aid and contraception.

The involvement of local agencies has found universal approval among young people and staff. Local agencies will generally be seen by teachers as having some special expert knowledge and experience on issues such as drugs and therefore will have a crucial role in helping young people, not only to explore the issues in an open way but to appreciate the part that voluntary and statutory organizations play in the life of the community.

Theatre in Education groups have also been invited to enrich the day's proceedings and pick up some of the themes that were addressed in the workshop sessions. These proved popular in helping to illustrate the issues in an accessible way.

SCHOOL INVOLVEMENT AND FEEDBACK

These conferences are expensive and labour-intensive. They do represent a partnership approach and the commitment by the school senior management is crucial to their success. They need to be prepared well in advance, with the full support of the school in arranging students into workshops. However, the evidence is that once the teachers observe the interest of the students they are more than willing to support the initiative. They feel that the time spent is worthwhile and, while in some cases teachers and students are reluctant to take time out from tight academic schedules, most see it as a creative break from the academic curriculum.

Conferences now are an integral part of the Personal, Social and Health Education curriculum at several schools. Facilitators welcome the chance to meet together beforehand to obtain help in devising the content of the session, and also for a debriefing session at the end of the conference.

One school devised an effective evaluation process. After the workshops students went back to their usual tutor groups and with the assistance of one of their peers discussed their experiences according to previously agreed questions. The representatives then met with the school organizers and facilitators to hear the feedback from the students. The facilitators were also able to express their experience of the groups. Such an interchange can be a moving experience for all. Comments included: 'Everyone enjoyed themselves and came away better equipped to face some of the things we come up with in life'; 'It was a quality combination of both education and entertainment'; 'We felt that the workshop leaders were easy to talk to and ready to listen'; 'The workshops gave people a chance to participate, the students took control and talked about what was important to them.' The fact that the conferences took place out of school was also welcomed. One comment that particularly helped a facilitator who thought perhaps he was a bit too old to be leading a workshop was that 'the speaker was on the same wavelength as us!' Also: 'There was no comeback, the discussion was good, we talked and got things we wanted to know'; 'We don't have to research and write essays about it, it happened, it was good, and it finished.'

These conferences are self-standing and do not necessarily have to be followed up in school; while such events cannot replace a sustained PSHE programme, they certainly add a dynamic dimension to the taught curriculum. (See also Appendix.)

SUMMARY

While organizers are conscious of involving facilitators who are not a lot older than the participants, it has been shown that having a large age mix can only enhance the quality of the event. People who have been involved in leading workshops will of course come from a wide range of differing organizations and care must be taken in the selection process, using personal recommendation; also, given concerns over child protection, organizers will want to be satisfied of the credentials of those recruited. Among professional and voluntary workers who have been involved are youth and community workers (full or part time), social workers, local university student welfare officer or president, drugs agency workers, staff from HIV/AIDS services, health promotion workers, family planning co-ordinator, community dieticians, St John's Ambulance workers, the Child and Family Consultation Service, housing advice workers and careers advice workers.

CONCLUSION

The theme of this chapter is the principle that young people should be central to the process of drugs education, no matter on what level of sophistication it is conducted, from the basic level of listening and conversing to the more structured and informal education approaches. The important element is that young people should be valued: not necessarily that their behaviour is condoned, but they are accepted in all cases as having something to offer. Starting with young people's expressed views and needs on drugs issues allows drugs educators to provide focused education and information, which is likely to have credibility in the promotion of healthier lifestyles among young people. There is nothing essentially new in the approaches suggested, but they do require time, energy and commitment, and there will be setbacks.

Some may argue that off-the-shelf programmes have clearer objectives and ideology and are likely to continue to be favourably received as providing the answer to the vexed question of young people's involvement with drugs.

However, what is likely to have more lasting effect is work that springs from a partnership between young people and adults, at all levels, where their experiences and views are incorporated into the activities that are adopted. This is likely to create more memorable moments and provide more enriching education and experiences, and therefore make a significant contribution in protecting and equipping young people in a drug-using world.

APPENDIX: HEALTH CONFERENCES FOR YOUNG PEOPLE

Summary of the action plan:

- Start planning one term in advance.
- Small group to meet with organizing teacher and student representatives to identify health issues of mutual concern.
- Budget projected. This must include facilitators' fees, catering and accommodation charges.
- Venue identified, e.g. youth centres, hotels, conference centres, teacher centres.
- Current productions from local theatre-in-education groups considered and bookings made.
- Workshop leaders identified using local networks through youth service, health authority, education and voluntary sector.
- Briefing meeting arranged; time, content and equipment needs specified.
- Details of workshops made available to school several weeks beforehand. Allow students to sign up for workshops in advance.
- Information point – perhaps organized in conjunction with local youth information project, health promotion etc.

On the day:

- Registration point.
- Conference pack for each student indicating times, locations of workshops etc. Stewards available to assist delegates to find rooms.
- Debriefing session at close of conference involving organizers, students and facilitators. Or individual evaluations completed and analysed later.
- Within a few weeks report prepared, sent to workshop leaders, school or youth organization management and presented to participants.

Other considerations:

● Funding: conferences could be jointly commissioned by education or
health authorities and the school or youth organization.

REFERENCES

Best, D.W., Mortimer, R.M., Davies, J.B. and MacMillan, D. (1995) *Fast
Forward Peer Research Project Evaluation Report.* Strathclyde: Centre for
Applied Social Psychology Strathclyde University.
Chamberlain, A. (1987) *Talking With Young People.* Health Action Pack
Background papers. London: HEA.
Chapman, C. (1995) *Drug Education: A Glimmer of Light Health Education
1.* Bradford: MCB University Press.
Clements, I. and Buczkiewicz, M. (1993) *Approaches to Peer Led Education: A
Guide for Youth Workers.* London: HEA.
Coffield, F. and Gofton, L. (1994) *Drugs and Young People.* London: London
Institute for Public Policy Research.
De Haes, W. (1987) Fifteen years exploration of the effects of different drug
education programmes. *Health Education Research Theory and Practice,*
2(4), December, 433–8.
Fast Forward (1993/4) *Sharing Works Annual Report.* Edinburgh: Fast For-
ward Positive Lifestyles Ltd.
Frankham, J. (1995). Peer education: are we taking things for granted? Paper
presented to the Trust for the Study of Adolescence Conference on Peer
Counselling/Peer Education, 12 May 1995.
Gordon, S. (1986) *Balancing Acts: How to Encourage Youth Participation.*
Leicester: National Youth Bureau.
Hirst, J. and McCamley-Finney, A. (1994) *The Place and Meaning of Drugs in
the Lives of Young People.* Health Institute Report No. 7. Sheffield: Sheffield
Hallam University.
O'Connor, L. (1995) Drug education in schools: getting it right. Paper pre-
sented to the London Drugs Policy Forum Conference, 24 March 1995,
Youth Culture – Drug Culture. London: Drugs Policy Forum.
O'Connor, L., Best, D.W., Best, R.M., Rowley, J. (1997) *Drugs Education in
Schools: Missed Opportunities.* London: Roehampton Institute London,
Merton, Sutton and Wandsworth Health Authority.
Parker, H., Measham, F. and Aldridge, J. (1995) *Drug Futures: Changing
Patterns of Drug Use Amongst English Youth.* Research Monograph No. 7.
London: ISDD.
Power, P., Power, T. and Gibson, N. (1996) Attitudes and experiences of drug
use amongst a group of London teenagers. *Drugs Education, Prevention
and Policy,* **1**(1).
Shiner, M. and Newburn, T. (1996) *Young People, Drugs and Peer Education:
An Evaluation of the Youth Awareness Programme (YAP).* Home Office
Drug Prevention Initiative Paper No. 13. London: HMSO.
Stewart, F. (1992) Youth policy in the 1990s. In Colman, J. and Warren
Adamson, C. (eds) *The Way Forward.* London: Routledge.

Concluding comments

Denis O'Connor and Louise O'Connor

Reading the contributions presented here can evoke interest, hope, concern, frustration. It all depends on the mind-set of the reader. If the reader seeks certainty, a clear unambiguous path to success, the likelihood is that he or she will be disappointed. The feeling may well be that events should have moved further on, clearly indicating the way forward. However, the fact is that we are only just working out the intelligence base for working together; identifying the fears and needs of parents; discovering how we can reach the young; and the limits of our effectiveness in schools.

Perhaps the most fruitful approach at this stage of our development is to regard where we have arrived as the first chapter in our *collective learning*. There is a well known model of learning (see Figure A) which describes progress.

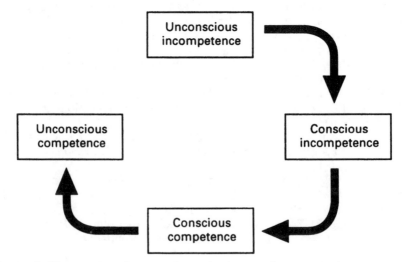

Figure A. Unconscious incompetence to unconscious competence.

The easiest analogy to illustrate the model is riding a bicycle, where the progress from incompetence to something that becomes second nature is clearest. Nevertheless, it is not unreasonable to plot our present progress at the 'conscious incompetence' stage. We have discovered a number of pieces of the jigsaw, and identified many gaps. We are concerned too with the potential 'lack of bite' both in individual key elements, for example the marginal effect of Circular 4/95 in schools, and in the uncertainties of DATs who doubt that they hold 'executive' authority. But at least we have arrived at the point where we can see the difficulties more clearly day by day. We can also, with increasing certainty, distinguish false starts and cul-de-sacs from mainstream development in education, health and enforcement.

We are wedded to a 'what works' approach, and this inevitably means focusing on approaches that are informed by research evidence, rather then the somewhat patchy, piecemeal efforts evidenced by high-profile initiatives which lack a convincing rationale. Thus we need to track the progress of DATs in achieving collective impact, and be prepared to review their terms of reference if, two years on, they are progressing slowly. We need also to share the intelligence model that is most likely to generate attention and action. Finally we need to capitalize on schools as centres not just of learning but of sustained community action to address the wider social context of drug use and misuse. Schools acting in concert with parents, health workers and police officers to reduce the acceptability and availability of drugs present a powerful opportunity to address the problems caused by drug misuse to young people, their families and their communities.

Name index

Subject index